Orphaned Words

Forgotten Poems from a Haphazard Life

* * *

RD Armstrong

©2018 by RD Armstrong

All rights reserved. No part of this book may be reproduced without the express written permission of the author, except in the case of written reviews.

ISBN 978-0-9984580-9-0

First edition

Library of Congress Control Number 2018902497

PO Box 5301
San Pedro, CA 90733
www.lummoxpress.com

Printed in the United States of America

Acknowledgments:
Most of these poems have not been published elsewhere… but a few have. The author thanks the editors who were savvy enough to see the value of these "orphaned" poems. The author also thanks LUMMOX Press for giving him an opportunity to reach such a unique audience. And finally, thanks to you, the readers, for your interest and support.

For more books of poetry, please visit the LUMMOX Press website.

Table of Contents

Foreword .... *viii*

3 Bucks 1
3 Line Bio 2
8:45 Tuesday a.m. 3
11-8-16 4
After the Reading 3 5
Against Cold Steel 6
Ambush 8
Am I Ok? 9
A Poem for the Exes 10
A Poem/Shovel 11
A Silver Line 12
A Stranger is Waiting 13
Aunt Rhoda's Last Request 14
Bargain 15
beat poet 16
Beavus 17
Benediction II 18
Beware the Ides of March 19
Birth of an Asshole 20
Blue Highway Redux 22
Blue Rock Meditation 24
Breath 25
Buffoon At Large 26
Building Blocks 28
Bungalows on De Longpre 29
Burning Man 30
Cast Iron 32
Chakra #4 33
Chet Baker 34
Cinco de Malo 35
Cold Fingers 37

> > >

Contents...

Consumer	38
Cool Blue Walls	39
Crazy 2	40
Creep	42
Cul-de-sac	43
Dark Days	44
Dilemma	45
Dogmah	47
Down for the Count	48
Dream	49
Dream: Sharks	50
Driving Home	52
Edgar Degas is Very Dead	53
Ethical concerns among the miserable	54
Fall in Long Beach	55
Fang	56
Fear of the Pen	57
Forks in a Jar	62
Frontline	63
Goodbye Margaret Mead	64
Gotta Get Right...	65
Guilt by Association	66
Hank's Fourth	67
Have I Told You About the Rain	68
Have You Heard this One?	69
Hiking the Rogue River Trail – 1972	71
Highwire Act	73
Hospital Sequence	74

   Abandonment Issues, Don't Lose Yo' Cool,
   Dream Catcher, Haunted House, Hospital Codes,
   Hospital Diet, Morphine Dreaming, Man's Burden,
   Nocturnal Obsession, Stir Crazy, The Foot,
   The Loneliest Feeling, On My Street,
   Green Thumb, Dire Consequences

Ice Cubes and Black Coffee	93
Ignorance	94
I Hate	95
I Knew Your God	96
I'm Tired	99
Immortal Lines	100
In the Shadow of the Jagged Moon	101
Invisible on Aisle 5	103
I Saw Yojimbo Today	106
I thought I was	107
It's My Own Fault	108
Ivy II	109
Jacaranda	110
La Puerta del Diablo	111
Leaf: Turning	112
Life on the Street	114
Lonely Girl	116
Lucid Thought #2	117
Maturity	118
Memorial Day	119
Missing You	121
My Head is a Soggy Sponge	122
New Year's Eve 2003	123
No Excuse For Domestic Violence	124
Number 7	125
Obligation	126
Odysseus Returned	127
On Growing Old	128
On Returning Home	129
On the Death of Mike Adams	130
On the Margin	131
One Finger at a Time	132
One for the Road	133
Outside the Zen Center	135
Poem	136

> > >

Contents...

Portrait	137
Rain Coming Down	139
Reality Check	140
Requiem for a Jazz Drummer	141
Red State Blues	143
Resistance	144
Road Rage	145
Sad and Lonesome Blues	146
Santa Ana	147
Sitting in my Bed	148
Slice of Life	150
Something that my Dream Mother Said	151
Something's Wrong Here	152
SOS	155
Spell Breaker	156
Stone	157
Stop	158
Strange in October	159
Street Zendo	160
Table Scraps	161
Tarnished Crown	162
Tears have No Color	163
Thanks	165
The Beast	167
The Bukowski Tour	168
The Curse	170
The Doormat's Revenge	171
The Eye Moves On	172
The Flower	173
The Fine Print	174
The Junk Man	176
The Lady Waits	177
The Liquid Daze	178
The Miracle of Birds	179
The Morning Chorus	180

The New Adventure - Aug. 2008	*182*
The Olympics	*184*
The Pin Cushion	*185*
The Poet from El Paso	*186*
The Quiet Revolution	*187*
The Road to Ruin	*188*
The Seed Lady	*190*
The Siren's Call	*191*
The Sloop	*192*
The Soon to Be Rapture	*194*
The Wages of Living	*197*
The Watcher	*198*
The Wolf at the Door	*199*
The World According to Diabetes	*200*
The Young Poet	*201*
Things I Notice #8	*202*
Tonight It's the Russian Children	*204*
Touch Me	*205*
Tough	*206*
Tran Zen Dance	*208*
Tyrannus Sexualis	*209*
Unnamed Act	*212*
Unleashing the Hound	*213*
Untitled	*214*
untitled 2	*215*
Untitled 3	*216*
Uprooted	*217*
Vacation	*218*
Water	*219*
What Unites Us	*220*
Witness	*221*
You	*224*
Zen-Fuck-You	*225*
About the Author	*229*

FOREWORD

BACK IN 2007, blissfully unaware of how much my life was about to change, I decided to publish a book of my selected poems 1993 to 2007. So I read through the 700 or so poems I'd written at that point and selected what I thought were my faves and ended up with about 300 poems! These I published in a two volume set, **Fire and Rain, 1 & 2** (I thought 300 + pages was a little presumptuous at the time, especially for a first full length collection). Prior to this, all my publications were chapbooks.

Then in 2008, just prior to the dramatic life-change, I published 3 of my "road trip" poems, one of which ran 61 pages! The book was entitled **On/Off the Beaten Path**. Finally, I published **El Pagano & Other Twisted Tales** (a collection of seriously bent short stories). There have been a few more titles over the years, all part of the ever-unfolding canon of my writing career... All of these books can be seen on my LUMMOX Press website.

Now, I have put together most of the "other" poems into this new volume. They represent the '*dirty laundry*', the poems that were ignored by all the previous titles, in short, *the forgotten poems*. I put this volume together because I learned a valuable lesson from one of the other titles that I put out back around 2011...and that was this, you never know what the reader will latch onto, be it your best or your worst! I realized that I had a lot of poems that I had denied to the general readership because *I* thought them sub-par. But really, who am I to judge?

The **Haphazard Life** mentioned in the title refers to the dramatic turn of events that set me off on this leg of the journey. I was working as a handyman/laborer/jack-of-all-trades and had done so for thirty years (my main income). I did okay, but it was a smallish life. I had been sober for almost 20 years - that was something I *was* proud of. Then in 2004, something broke inside me...I began drinking again (like a fish), as if I was trying to make up for my best behavior by unleashing the hounds of hell! Sadly, in this day and age, it's not remarkable, many have experienced it; though as relapses go, it was pretty damn harsh, to my way of thinking! I spun effortlessly out of control for four more years, until late in 2008 when I entered a hospital (for the first time since I was born) with a septic ulcer on the heel of my right foot. This was to be the beginning of my immersion into the health care machine. When they told me I was diabetic, I quit drinking (but really, I just substituted the drug of alcohol for the many drugs required to maintain a Diabetic). I was 57 years old.

Another factor that should be mentioned here is that I sincerely thought I would be dead by 60. This turned out to be a misconception, a colossal one! My father had always worried about growing older and somewhere along the line I got this idea that his father had died in *his* 60's. Turns out my grandpa was at least 20 years older than I thought, in his 80's. As a result of my poor intel, I never put much away for savings *and* didn't put much into my social security… why put in the money if I'd never be able to use it? There's an old saying: "you've made your bed, and now you have to sleep in it!"

It was one of my more bone-headed moves, not the worst, but in the top ten!

Ten years later and I no longer work with tools of a manual labor nature. I squeak by selling other people's poetry books and from the modest Supplemental Income check I get every month -- it's a spartan lifestyle at best, but it's the life I chose. I made a mistake, now I must make it work because I have no other choice. Nobody cares if I fail, but I'm not prepared to fall through the cracks just yet. I'm working on making my last decade something to be remembered (besides being the biggest damn fool ever!)

My life has become bigger because of my renewed sobriety and because of the **LUMMOX Press** (my publishing outfit   > > >

Foreword… which has intensified production over the past five years because I need to make money). If it weren't for LUMMOX Press, I'd be living out of my car, drunk on my ass and crazy. As it is, I'm the quirky/eccentric geezer who's always quick with a joke or a snarky remark…trying to make my way in my "golden [shower] years" without a parachute to cushion my landing (it's fortunate that I couldn't afford a ticket on the plane and that thing I keep yanking on, thinking it's the rip-cord, is actually a thread on the rapidly unraveling sweater that is my life).

Yes, it's been ten years of poking and prodding and almost a million dollars worth of medical expenses (medications, two 14 day stays in hospital, countless blood draws, one toe amputation, doctors both good and bad, xrays, MRIs, skin cancers, ups and downs)…a very full decade, medically speaking.

With that as background, I'm still trying to excel, both with my eccentricities, my writing and my poetry business. It's an impossible dream…a helluva Vienna, but here I am, still.

I hope that you, the reader, will find some of this poetry of value, either as entertainment or perhaps, as an unexpected illumination that clarifies some aspect of your life, as well. If that's the case, then I've done my job.

RD Armstrong
Long Beach, CA
March, 2018

The Orphans

3 Bucks

She hands me three moist one dollar bills
I take them, gingerly and place them in my wallet
"Thanks" She says seductively
"Uhuh." I reply
I'm ashamed that I can't make eye contact with her
I know that she'll take it as a sign of greater importance
than it would be intended
I'm often misunderstood by women
My friendliness is mistaken for something
more and there is never an easy explanation
because they think *they* know
but they don't
How could they, how
could anyone?

Hell, I don't even know

3 Line Bio

"Just send a short bio, three lines or so."

Ain't gone to prison yet
Poor, single and living in Long Beach
No, Raindog is not my real name

8:45, Tuesday a.m.

"I considered suicide until
I remembered the taste of fruit"

Hearing these words on the radio
as I wait to inch into the number four
lane on the ten-east,
my lips still aching from your
hungry kisses;
I glide into traffic
wearing your scent
like a second skin,
the taste of Mt. Fuji apples
lingering on my tongue,
and my cock, still aroused, longing to return
to the warmth of your bed,
to penetrate you
like a blade being driven home.

11-8-16

the old man
recalls
it was like
a cheap shot
to all of the
chacras
simultaneously.
After I got
over it
I went back
to waiting
for the muse
to bathe me in
poetry.

After the Reading 3

I recently attended
A reading in Ventura County
For the twenty-second
Anniversary of ArtLife
I was invited to read
Along with numerous
Other poets of local fame
I noticed the guys my
Age were reading poems
About the pleasures of
Love and family life
I read a nature poem
At times like these
I am reminded
(Particularly around this
Time of year) of the
Absence of home and hearth
Of kith and kin
The warmth of fellowship
Not everyone is so blessed
There was a time
When I knew these blessings
But that time is all but forgotten
Now I'm grateful for the chance to
Warm my hands at the fire
Even if it isn't in my true home
Or with my true family
One learns to adapt
If one wants to survive

Against Cold Steel

I used to have a chair
a chrome thing from the 50s
with a tattered and beaten
green vinyl covering.
I found it with its twin
in the alley behind where
I live now, two doors down.
It was very comfortable.
Now I use one of those
ergonomically correct things.
It's supposed to be better on
the back/posture but to be honest
it hurts my knees after a while.
The old chair never made my
knees sore, but sometimes my
feet would fall asleep.
Now my posture is good
and the women all think I'm
hung like a horse because I
walk around with an easy,
self-assured grace.
I'm nobody's fool and I know it.

I miss my old chair.
It had class.
Sure, it was old and kind of
beat up (much like myself).
Maybe it wasn't as pretty as
this black metal machine
with its cute, little black castors
and its gray twill fabric on the
seat and knee rest.
But this modern chair is
soul-less and has all the appeal
of a clean line or a mirrored wall.

I'm going to switch it for my
old chair right now.
Ahhhhh.
There. Now I can crack my neck
and feel the odd warmth of my
legs against cold steel at last.

Life begins to make sense again.

AMBUSH

I just wrote my first poem of the new year.
It had its moments
but I'm not worried
since these things tend
to start up slowly
fitfully like an old
truck on a cold day
or an old man getting
out of bed.

Next month I start
my creep down the
backside of the hill

Maybe fifty will be
a banner year for me
after all but if it is
anything like forty-nine
it will dart past me
like a startled mouse

Mostly I hope that
I will release the ideas
that are presently
banging around inside
my head like ricocheting
bullets with my sanity
caught in the cross-fire

AM I OK?

(Found poem in an email message from "The Geeze")

Of course not.
The world is in chaos
and I want physically to
fight bigotry and insanity
with a Howitzer.
I want to use violence and
scream at my closest neighbor.
I want everyone to leave Los
Angeles so I
can run the Freeways naked.
No! I am not okay.
I am looking for peace and
finding cyclical History.
I am looking for justice
from an election stolen
from my progressive hopes.
I am looking for cohesion
of religion, oneness
in thought, a lifting of my head.

No I am not okay

A Poem For The Exes

Every dog has his...
So the popular line
of wisdom states
And
Hemingway had his...
at least until the
cheers faded
And
you've had mine
at least as much
as I've had yours
and still
we walk the
face of this
dirt clod

All the laundry
and dirty dishes
flowers and notes
of apology
cheap wine and easy lies
will not change that
Nor will the struggle
of these few simple lines

not to you
not to me
not to any
of us.

Carumba!

A POEM/SHOVEL

A poem does not
have to be a shovel
stick of dynamite
bullet hole
fist closing around your throat
or even the unblinking eye of death

A poem can be rude
shocking
thought-provoking
boring
just by stating the obvious
differently

A poem can be a table
chair
door
window
tree
fence
night
day
sun
moon
your loving eyes
your hateful eyes
a gaping mouth
a tight-lipped mouth
head
hands
belly
chest
heart

A poem is everything
and nothing
forever & never.

A Silver Line

A silver line
a chalk streak
really
hangs in the
velvet darkness

It could be a silhouette
of a man in 3/4 profile
or it could be
a string of hopes
unraveling
like the plans of
men and mice

Assume it is the man
what's he up to?
what scheme will he
dream of hatching next?
what will the spot light
reveal when it next opens on him?

The man dreams of
his release from the
bitter taste that lingers
in the mouth after
one dines on crow

Even as the profile is discovered
the man ceases to exist
a theater of smoke and mirrors
that collapses at the slightest
breath of reality

A Stranger Is Waiting

It's said that
The perfect mate is out
There waiting to be found
But what if you've already
Missed them or worse
What if you've already
Blown it with that
Person; what if you zigged
When you should've zagged or
Turned the wrong corner and
Someone else is bumping into
Your "life-mate" as this is
Being written
What about that?

AUNT RHODA'S LAST REQUEST

My dad's brother
my uncle John
is going to drive from Arizona
to the Tetons in Wyoming
(that's near Jackson Hole)
to scatter his wife's ashes to
the winds.

It was her last request.

After years of following him from one
"hole-in-the-wall" to the next
(all over the western states)
she's finally going to get him to do
something for her
(Besides take out the trash).
It's so romantic and
so much a part of the western tradition
like the last scene in the movie
"The Searchers"

I get a lump in my throat every time I think about it.

Bargain

The assassin stood close by   love
as the two lovers embraced   honor
on the porch of the young   cherish
woman's home. Hearts raced   for
as fate drew the three together   as long
the lovers and the hater.   as you
Three lives   both
ruined: shall
the hater and the lovers   live

It was a cruel efficiency
that sent two young
lovers to heaven and
one to hell that fateful
afternoon last week in
North Long Beach.
One bullet: three lives.

up

beat   poet

down

BEAVUS

My friend showed me pictures
of his sister naked and fucked
up on some shit. He probably
stole (or bought) them from her
ex-husband – he'd do *anything
for a buck, except work.* I stared
at those rumpled photos with a
kind of morbid fascination, like
when you slow down and gawk
at an accident. There was his
sister buck naked on a bed
playing with her goodies.
There she was on her knees,
looking back over her shoulder
towards the camera, a lurid grin
snaking across her face. There
she was cupping her breasts in
each hand, looking up at the
camera, her face, slightly out of
focus, mouth open,
eyes like slits, waiting for
the sacramental reward.
My friend showed me his sister
fucked up and horny. Each time
I flipped to a new photo he giggled
like Beavus the cartoon guy. If you
have seen the movie Deliverance,
you will understand my friend a little
better. His people come from the hills
above Los Angeles, over by Sierra
Madre. I think maybe the hill folk are
the same everywhere you go.
That was many years ago. My friend's
sister moved away and I dare not try
to see her again. She can't know of
my guilty secret. How can I explain
to her why I catch my breath if ever
she might smile at me as she looks
back over her shoulder.

BENEDICTION II

I want to fill my mouth
With your angry words
That hover like stale smoke
Laden air, chewing on them,
Mashing and crushing them,
Mixing the broken syllables and
Violent vowels with my own saliva,
Absorbing the last bits of nutrition
From them before i spit the
Dead bones of this absurd
Hatred to the ground
To shatter and turn
To dust and blow away!

I want to hear the
cries of these streets, rising like
startled birds in a chorus
of anguish and suffering,
scattering across the skyline,
obscuring the sun, itself,
as the howling pain of
generations eclipses and
overpowers the roaring
sound from even the
blast furnaces of hell!

Fill me like a sack,
fill me until my seams
begin to split and i can't
hold anymore and then,
mercifully, drop me into
the deepest hole around
and wipe your hands
and walk away.

Beware the Ides of March

I hung a shirt up in the bathroom
to dry out. It was dark blue and
kind of bulky. Every time I had to
go into the bathroom to do some-
thing I'd have to duck under it to
get in and I would vaguely recall
an event that took place many years
ago. It was in 1977 when I lived in
the South Bay the memory that is.
A student of mine found his father
hanging in the bathroom hung by a
lamp cord from a pipe overhead. He
had been depressed. My student's
mother told him that it was an
accident but I don't think he ever really
believed her. I don't know why the
shirt is triggering that memory
I never saw the actual suicide tableau.
I do acknowledge that I've got a full
plate with many irons in the fire and
a head full of ideas that are driving
me insane but this is not new...

BIRTH OF AN ASSHOLE

It took me a long time to realize
But when I finally got
the message
it was so obvious
that I didn't know whether to cry or
to laugh.
I chose to laugh
I laughed
I laughed so hard
I laughed so hard I split the seat
out of my pants
and then
I laughed some more
I laughed at all the years
I wasted being wasted
trying to conceal
to cover-up
to hide
All the years of guilt
and denial
Spent in the closet
All the confusion
spent dreams
misguided ideals
Moments of illumination
quickly and hurriedly
concealed
All the wasted drunks
trying to be clever
All the morning afters spent
apologizing
NEEDLESSLY
All the time spent backtracking
FOR NOTHING

All those years bunching up to form the mother of all wedgies
in the ultimate cosmic plumbers crack
The light of inspiration illuminates best
when you raid the ice-box of your soul at 3 AM
looking to snack on some philosophical morsels
Or you're merely talking on the phone
and the standard line of bullshit
takes a sudden unexpected turn.

Blue Highway Redux

Down at the Crossroads
a big yellow dog waits patiently
as if divine inspiration will strike
at any moment.
It does not and the dog
meanders off towards Memphis
but works its way back
along the Arkansas side of the road.

Clarksdale in late August
is awash in a tropical mist
that causes the bravest souls
to shrink into the cool
air-conditioned darkness of
any tavern or juke joint in town.
Across wooden floors
polished with age
with the naked imprints
of generations
across these cool boards
she moves
barefoot
the hem of her dress
dancing at her ankles
like a thousand birds rising to flight
reeling to and fro
flashing from light to dark
to light again
and still she comes
on feet as strong as
the desire to work this land
feet as brown as the soil
fecund and moist with life's
sweet potential

and still she comes
as if coming in from the fields
as if rising like spring floodwaters
seeking the crest
reclaiming what was once hers
and still she comes
proud and graceful
stately like a grand and noble cause
like an idea who's time has come
she has arrived
stand back and give her room

Now she calls the tune
she has come to dance.

BLUE ROCK MEDITATION

clouds wash across western slopes
scrubbing spring's shaggy beard
grooming sage and thistle and
arranging Autumn's lonely bed.

Catalina floats serenely
above blue pacific waters
on this day in
late spring
like Godzilla
waiting to pounce
on unsuspecting oil barges
floating
match-box like
in the narrows.

the spires of downtown L.A.
on fire in late afternoon
like booster rockets
pushing Mt.
Baldy into orbit
its nosecone
still white with last
month's dusting.

blue rocks cupping
this basin like
arms
forming the San Berdoo
the Santa Ana's
hands
with fingers spread wide
making canyons
and valleys
reaching into
dancing blue waves.

BREATH

1.
As I play my flute
You dance in my heart
and the notes   float away
                                            like dreams
returning
to the bamboo forests
of their birth.

2.
watching you walk away
I think of the last
blast of air escaping
Lester Young's horn.

3.
hyper-ventilating
I float above

my breath
waiting for it to r
                        i
                   s
                      e
                            to meet me

Buffoon At Large

So this is what it comes down to
Trapped in a world that
I neither understand nor
Belong to.

Relegated to the over-sized peanut gallery
Trading quips with the half blind
And the overly clever
Vying for the attentions
And hopelessly outclassed by
Ladies of interest
Who would just as soon walk away
As give me the time of day.

And yet
For a brief shining moment
There is the illusion of interest
Even if feigned
Even if it's only a
Pretend moment
That I cannot explain

As I watch *Reality Shows* and do not
Share this reality
Knowing I have let slip from my grasp
The standard line of American credit:
House
Family
New car
Brave new world
As I watch the cult of personality
And cannot feel anything for Russell
Or Brad and Jen
Tom and Katie

Lindsey and her paparazzi stalkers
Much less George W. and his drooping
Numbers or the growing war dead
Or Michael J. and his ailing back
Africa and China
Police overreactions or
The decline of everything we hold near and dear.

I only have my non-standard existence
My solitary groove
My brief moments of connectivity
From my perch
In the gallery of buffoons
Where the one liner is all I have
All that is expected of me
The easiest way through the door

Don't let the nose fool you
I am no clown
Buster
It's just make-believe

Building Blocks

Stupidity drips from
the walls of my "house"
It is wallpaper
plaster
paint
lath
framing
plumbing
gas line
wiring
It is shingle
and tar paper
it is glass and brick
door and sash
carpet and concrete
Stupidity glares back at me
over the sink
it mutters under its breath
at the foot of the stairs
it pisses on the trash can
of intelligence
Stupidity lingers
on my breath like a green
onion toxic cloud
it crawls up my leg
in the dark aftermath of
"one more day"
(with/without)
Stupidity is the door
I must go through
everyday at least once every hour.
It is the barrier of atoms
that separates me from
desire
and a world I
pretend to understand
but do not.

Bungalows on De Longpre

The bungalows on De Longpre
do not sing a happy tune
do not stand out like a vase of
happy yellow flowers w/
brown faces and radiant petals

The bungalows on De Longpre --
a skidmark off of Normandie
in the cracked stucco jungle
of east Hollywood
Walls stained w/ the rust
of Lorca's tears, of grieving widows
at the gates of paramount studios
standing at the intersection of the
avenida de los lost souls and the parque
of the disappeared w/ crumpled renderings
of lost familia pleading w/ red eyes and
tear-stained cheeks for hope or charity

The bungalows on De Longpre
do not speak a known language but
mumble in a dialect inaudible except to dogs:
sounds like bones being slowly crushed
by a large stone wheel

The bungalows on De Longpre
looking tedious and unrepentant
on a Saturday afternoon in humorless sunshine
standing like monuments to the War All The
Time of 1966 Los Angeles and the sweet
miracle of words ratcheted loose
from the yawning mouth of death
and nailed to the page by the clackity-clack
of a drunken two o'clock in the morning typewriter.

BURNING MAN

I am building a statue
in my secret desert
out of the cast-offs of woman-kind
the debris forming
a forty foot man
like the one in the Nevada desert
that the hippies and cyberpunks burn every year
and like that other man
mine, too, will be torched
by some fool with a zippo

"My boyfriend's blah blah blah..."
It's always the same
I don't know what it is about me,
but the women just want to confide in me
no, they NEED to confide in me
to tell me all the juicy tid-bits

I guess they figure to be doing me a favor
by allowing me to enrich my fantasy life
with their saucy little vignettes
And they DO form quite a patchwork quilt
of memories and fantasies
the patterns blending and merging
so that in my old age
I won't be able
to tell truth from fiction.

And they bring me their stories wrapped
in the sacred cloth of their vitality
their excited ripeness
dancing around me as though I was their maypole
swirling around me like tropical fish
all neon against the azure sea,

eyes flashing with passion,
electric and inflamed
frenzied
breathless
wide-eyed
and innocently sensual.

But perhaps,
someday I will stop listening
to their stories
and BECOME the story myself
and their tongues can wag about me!

CAST: IRON

Each of us sits
in our respective
heaven or
hell,
in a Destiny bath tub
we float in our own juices
glowering or glowing
depending
on chance
or the emperor's
mood

CHAKRA #4

"and the crowd is but a tinkling of voices where there is no love."
—e. e. cummings

The heart
Like the shark
Is an indiscriminate predator
It selects its prey using an occult science
That is still so mysterious most researchers
Have given up understanding the process and
Have moved on to less complicated fields of study
Such as Molecular Biology or Quantum Physics
While the heart in its infinite wisdom
Continues to plumb the depths of
Its mystery seeking a satisfactory answer
To the age old *WHY*?

Chet Baker

comes to mind,
his horn and his sadness
weaving a tale of
wistful melancholy
Not sorrow, per-Se
but a quiet introspection
unadorned with the hoo haa
and trappings of
emotionalism
that the modern world
requires for validity.
You were my Mother Theresa
touching me there
in my hour of depravity
giving me back my dignity
by simply reminding me
of my humanity.
I would return this
blessing to you
return it threefold
if I could find your
phone number.

CINCO DE MALO

Years ago,
on a night like this one
I gave up the ghost
the whole father/son thing
Holy trinity - WHATEVER!
I just didn't give a shit anymore...
about that brotherhood of the grape BLAH BLAH
the sweet wine of youth (double BLAH! BLAH!)
that Fante wrote about
that Bukowski lived so convincingly for
that all the big boys lobbied
so hard and so long for...
and shit was everywhere
everything was turning into watery shit
like thin red blood
so thin that you could count the corpuscles
hardly the Sangre de Cristo
I felt like I was drowning in an inch of bloody wine
like a moth doing the backstroke in a wine glass
And Oh how my glass raneth over!

I just gave up caring about any of that
It was taking far too long to do with the wine
what could be done with a bullet
so easily
and so finally
and
so what?!
BLAH was my mantra
and it colored all my days until passion was locked away and
desire lay with it's feet in the air
like a dead songbird
its melody forgotten
Fingers listlessly played at the frets   > > >

of a dead guitar without intention
The wind rustled the trees
and the electric meter ground on
relentlessly
marking time.

Desire lay sullenly
like scum on the surface of dead water
Eyes rolling like spilt olives
seeking direction
tongue presses teeth
mind searching for excuses
an explanation
a way out

I couldn't look myself in the eye
but could always count on that one last toast
before lights out.

Desire faded away
like sleep
like days melting into months
and months blurring into years
Time became something to waste and
Mechanism and routine took over

It was very bad
but then
it always is
before the storm breaks.

COLD FINGERS

of wind run through my hair
and sting my eyes
coaxing tears from
the corners like
shy prize fighters
unwilling to acknowledge
the bell.

Since you doused
me with gasoline and
burned down
my world
I have not been able
to feel anything
but the cold
wind
like fingers
gripping my heart
squeezing it
into stillness

CONSUMER

I am slowly replacing my blood
with coffee, 12 oz's a shot
which I consume like the sacred
blood of Jesus.

My breasts are filling out nicely
thanks to a steady diet of Fast Food
laced with steroids and estrogen
hormones.

My susceptibility to STDs and other
communicable diseases is progressing
according to plan since I started
drinking the tap water and swimming
in the harbor again.

Thanks to my dependence on TV
and my computer
my eyes are close to failing
my sperm are close to being
declared an endangered species
and there's a strange mass growing
on the side of my head.

At least the foil helmet is finally
blocking out the messages from
space-central command and I can
again understand what the voices
in the wall are trying to tell me to do.

Cool Blue Walls

Keith Jarrett was on the piano
a solitary chord
being endlessly dissected
Modern Jazz Fugue in B flat
the miserable serenity of
a voluntary poverty
flooding through my life
a river of dreams
breaking thru the barriers of
waking
unconscious blending with conscious
like the two Niles

Keith Jarrett at the helm
I on the couch
daydreaming
waiting for better days
to kick in the front door.

Crazy 2

I can't get the image out of my head:
the body of a young man
his naked white skin
now blue and ghost-like
a scene of Can-Can girls
high-stepping in gay abandon
replacing his genitals-
painted out-
or perhaps it is
Magrite's Blue Sky and White Cloud
His jeans stripped away
the fly torn loose and sent
to hang in the Louvre.

The awful image haunts me
the silver collar and bristles
barely visible
from his asshole
Death!
by paintbrush

The image walks the streets by night
prowling the darkened recesses of
my brain, unable to
dominate my mind
and bring me into it's satanic loop
but still strong enough to invade my
every dream
my every whim
every vision
There is no filter fine enough
to halt its infiltration
or ease its poisonous intent.

I can only rage against it
and pass myself off as one of you
But do not be mistaken
for I am not
one
of you.

Creep

The little man creeps up beside me
and asks for something
He always wants something
His need is epic
unsatisfyable
beyond
fulfillment
He pesters and cajoles me
until I surrender to his
onslaught
until I yield to his demands

And then he is gone
but tomorrow or the next day
or sometime when I don't really need
to be harassed
he'll return
for more of the same
more of something

Cul-de-sac

Coming to the end of another
short-cut
I am again
confronted by
the old demon
                doubt
Will I ever
pass beyond this point
or will I return
here,
cycling thru,
again and again
unable to break this
deja vu?

Dark Days

Sometimes I can't help myself
The anger boils up
From outta nowhere
And there's nothing I can do about it
Don't give me that
What'd I do look
When you know damn well that you walked
Through my world
Without permission
Smiled your knowing smile
(I don't care if you were just being polite)
And left me stranded on the corner of
Whatsit and shaboomy streets
With my hands in my pockets
Fishing for a token to catch
The next bus outta here

Best keep your hands inside
The ride at all times

Who knows what the animals
Will do if provoked

DILEMMA

Coming into this world late
I find it impossible to
keep up with all the
correspondence.

I never said, "I've got
nothing but free time"
but the message went out
somehow
and now I've got nothing
but free time to deal with
the mechanics of my art
the breaking down and
reconstructing of the
work of others.

I sleep with poets
but I come alone.
The poets I refer to are
present in the sheets
of poems that litter my
apartment
waiting like beggars
with hands outstretched
waiting for the alms
of publication. I do
what I can for them
they are my children
I cannot just turn away
I have a "responsibility"
it says so in Poet's Market

How did I get here?
(if you know the words
sing along)

> > >

Worst of all
I have to 'sneak' time
to do this – this
yes this writing
my own poems that I
will burden some other
editor with
At last
I see my revenge.
Ah and it feels good.

Okay play time is over.

DOGMAH

This grunting
squatting
process
of squeezing out
the words
rewards very little

only
a dry
stinkless
(if that's possible)
turd

Poet means "to make"
What good is poetry
if all you make
is shit
that don't
even
smell bad?
Shit that
don't
affect
anyone
for better
or worse.

DOWN FOR THE COUNT

It's a slippery slope
This side of the hill
How long you last
Determined not by
Any accounting
Known to man
But by random acts
Of the blinded fates

The only miracle
That can distinguish
You from the rest of the
Scrambling herd
Is the grace with
Which you cross the
Finish line

Dream

I live in a time where the agents of mercy
dispense justice without compassion,
honor or knowledge

Where the people grow weary of
living in fear,
caught in the middle of
a war of attrition.

This war is fought on many fronts
but the victims are always the same
and there is no escaping
the horrible price
of fear

except through the salvation of oblivion.

I live in a time where greed
overrules honor
where power is the god to be worshiped
and honored
where the tribute to that god is paid in blood
by the agents of retribution

And yet
within this climate of hatred
in the shadow of the cult of the gun
there are still the moments
of beauty when the whole
crazy madness and roar
of one life freezes for a few moments
and the fragrance of a sweeter life
like the scent of Gardenias or
fresh baked bread
caresses your troubled brow
pulling you from the nightmare
with an invitation to
the dream.

Dream: Sharks

I used to have this dream about sharks / every now and then / it wasn't a pleasant dream / nor a nightmare / just somewhere in between // it always starts out innocently enough / azure seas / crystal clear waters / fish / coral / the whole Lloyd Bridges thing / but as I looked down / deep / I began to see murky shapes / moving back and forth / gray and sinister / creepy // shark attack / barely escaping from my lips / sharks everywhere / hammer-heads / great whites / leopard sharks / sharks of every kind / color / shape / swimming back and forth / in that lazy / nonchalant way that they do / rising towards the surface / cold dread at legs / dangling // the dreams started when I was 18 or 19 // the psychological gang / leaping upon this dream / as a pack of hungry / dogs / its meanings / ignoring the simplicity / the fact that no shark ever took a bite / nibble / of my tootsies / dangling / tantalizing / a yummy fruit waiting to be plucked // the surrealism of the dream / lazy circles / seemingly innocent / I never was afraid / in the dream / foreboding / yes / but fear came in the waking / state / not dream / state // in retrospect / recollection / rationalization / explanation / the logic of fear / came / not in the dream / state // in the dream / state / I am floating on the skin of the sea / suspended between / heaven / earth / drifting / clueless / just me / me / me / unaware of the danger / my rendezvous with destiny / a destiny that wasn't scary / a destiny that was as threatening as a warm bath // in the explanation / I lose the essence of the dream / the knowledge and understanding / the power of the dream // the dream is a meditation / the I in the explanation / isn't doing / the dreaming / the I in the dream / exists within the / dream // floating / notice sky / horizon / waves / rippling shadows / glimmering light / pockets of shadow / fish / wavy looking legs / murky waters below / sharks / the multitude / swimming / minding our business / they / me // nothing ever happens / back in my 'right' mind the I makes up a reasonable fear /

makes / up / fearful explanation // years later / remembering the / dream / wondering / how many worries / woes / dreams lost / to practicality? / to rationalization? / convenient excuses / how many dreams / lost / to being / adult? // long before I learned / my dream sharks / were nothing compared to / those I would meet on / dry land / those sharks / the shredders / bottle-sharks / tight jean-sharks / naked at dawn-sharks / 20 to a pack-sharks / pain killer-sharks / 40 hour-sharks / back stabbing-sharks / egotistic-sharks / jingoistic-sharks / for-your-own-good-sharks // I'm awake / I think / now but / I can't escape the memory of / the dream ///

Driving home from the bar

I notice the trees look
More tree-like
And the streets look
More street-like
And the pedestrians
Look more pedestrian
And what the hell
Am I doing?

Nothing has changed
It all looks the same

Only I have changed.

Edgar Degas Is Very Dead

I saw a bag floating
in the sky
today
At first I thought
it was a crow
frozen in
the air but then
it moved
like a piece of
drifting ash.
I remembered that
Edgar Degas
is very dead
and the eye
of the crow
is yellow.

Ethical Concerns Among The Miserable

The first day after
I ran into my friend
Outside his favorite haunt
Well how's it going? says I
What? I can't hear you says he
Then he tells me about a
Drunken fist fight down at
The same beach where twenty
Years ago he'd lost the
Hearing in one ear when he
Was run over by a car
Drunk then too
Now he can't hear out of either ear
Now he feels miserable
Knowing what he lost then

And now he wants me to kill him
He seriously wants me to get a gun…
He's too afraid to do it himself
But doesn't mind sharing the
Misery with me
As if I don't already
Have enough of my own
Why won't you help me?
I thought you were my friend ?
To which I wonder I thought
YOU were my friend!
Only a dead Russian playwright
Could have written this any better

Fall in Long Beach

It was one of those rare moments
Where you just happen
To be paying attention to
Something besides yourself
And you notice that the
Neighborhood is
Quiet
Just the wind
In the trees and
Nothing else
And just for a few seconds
Or maybe a minute or so
You think "AHHH!"
THIS IS NI…
And then some car comes
And somebody starts a saw
And there it goes
That beautiful
Stillness

FANG

Jesus is dead
So is Art and Chet and Zoot and Joe and Django and Leonard and Hank
and Dusty and Brian and Jimi and Jim and Janis and John and Martin
and Bobbie and Ruben and Ceasar and Jerry and Frank and Zooey
and Cindy and Virginia and The Hawk and Albert and now
the ex calls me up to tell me that our youngest cat, Bear, is also gone
leaving only Franny
old
and frail
and who pisses all over
the house

(Still showing a bit of fang
even unto death)

When my time comes
may I be so lucky.

FEAR OF THE PEN

When I was younger
and wilder
in certain ways
I fancied myself
an authority on
the "PROCESS"
it was one of those
user friendly
expressions
coined by
the Humanist
School of
Psychology
the SELF help
introspective
native
intelligence gang.
The process is how
one lives
the way one
functions
and reacts
and in understanding
the process
one learned that life
is a fluid
evolving
transient
proposition
NOT a task to be
completed
cataloged
BUT a procession of
experiences linked

> > >

together by one's
particular twist of the
DNA ladder
interfacing with
the world.
The Process also
meant coming to grips
with one's place in one's time
owning one's impact.
It's not fashionable nowadays
in this world obsessed
with excuses
with assigning blame
with denials of responsibility
with political correctness
with the INDIVIDUAL
with blind allegiance
to god
country
MTV.
I thought I was in the
driver's seat
controlling
destiny
armed with the
knowledge of
process.
Part of knowing the
process was the
JOURNAL
in which I recorded
my thoughts
observations
occasional

moments of insight
lucid thought
but mostly the
journal became part of
the CON.
I explored the con
every angle
every scenario
realizing at last
that ultimately
I was SCUM
believing that I
was protected from
the stain of scum and
scummy actions
because I thought I
knew myself.
I wrote myself into a
cul-de-sac keeping
accurate notes of
the fall from grace
spanning three years
filling three journals.
I dropped like Icarus
hitting the ground
with the force of a
plummeting jetliner
scattering my possessions
for miles.
Friends fell away
scurrying for cover
lovers lost interest
forsaken
forgotten by   > > >

family
the things I valued
now clutter
broken and abandoned.
I clung to scattered pages
of my journals hoping
to insulate myself from the
cold
hard
reality of the
crater I now called home.
Soon the comfort of
the words
thoughts
delusions
began to cling to me
like shrink-wrap
crushing me like a dying son
collapsing in on him-self.
The tighter the squeezing
the more I believed I was
betrayed by friends
by family
by lovers
a very long list
negated by the
realization that the
biggest betrayer of all
was ME.
Oh the humanity
oh the shame
the craven denial
the weakness.
Now it's 34 years later

I'm still struggling to
live with my self-betrayal
my scummy side
my imperfections
my odd notoriety
my haters
my lovers.
No longer a journal-ist
I have found solace in
the written word
the wonder of insight
found in a simple
broken phrase
the power of using a
mental image to shine a
light on grace
or degradation
to illuminate the
mysteries of the
PROCESS.
I still distrust my
ability to chronicle
the process.
To some degree I
still fear the pen but
I have learned that
like the sword
it's the mind that
directs the hand as to
how it will be used.

Forks in a jar

When I first met you
In that funky clapboard
Two story house in
Hermosa
Living your vaguely
Simple life
A young mother on
Her own with two
Young children in tow
And I a hopelessly
Screwed up young man
Who fell for you
On that mid-week
Afternoon so many
Years ago

Now it is only a vague
Memory
More of an
Ache than anything else
Triggered by my habit
Of placing utensils
In glass jars
Just like you did

Frontline

The war
That no one expected
The war
That wouldn't end
Lies
Manipulation
4000 and counting
Corruption
And more lies
God damned liars
Cynical abandonment
The American Dream
Melting pot
Second rate power
God bless you
George Bush
Purveyor and
Pimp for avarice
And greed
The not-so almighty
Dollar as our new
God

A mound of earth
Next to a freshly dug grave
In Arlington Cemetery

The new moral high ground

Goodbye Margaret Mead

In a moment of desperation
I sold half of my library to the local used book store
It was a rash decision for which I will
feel guilty the rest of my days.
I felt as bad as if I had given my
children away
just to put a few morsels of food into my fat little mouth
A meal can sustain a hungry belly for a few days, at most
but a few well written ideas can sustain a hungry mind for years
(what exactly is the calorie to word ratio?)
Now when I go in there
and see copies of my old books
it's like visiting the orphanage where my
soon-to-be adopted children
now live.
Slowly
they are being purchased and
given new homes
where they will be honored
and cared for far better than I ever could.

In this life of "Cash & Carry"
selling books to buy food isn't much of a crime
but this is little consolation for me
as I wonder where all my children
have gone to.

Gotta Get Right...

To be honest,
I'm always in a daze, with
one foot tentatively in this world,
one foot somewhere else.

Lately I've had little energy,
dragging through each day without the crutch of drug or death to lean on,
no excuses,
no explanation,
merely wasting away under the dim bulb,
another burnout,
another flickering neon sign (sparking like a bug lamp)...
struggling against the sinister knowledge: last remembered, first forgotten;
drawing to an inside straight and placing a final bet before folding.

A distant train horn,
the desperate pock-a-ta-pock-a of a weapon discharging,
the insistent drone of LBPD copters overhead;
the whole neighborhood inflamed and suffering
while I nervously await the angel of mercy to invite me
to join the melee below and receive the holy sacrament
in all its steel-jacketed perfection.

Guilt By Association

Terry Schaivo is dead
John Paul the second
Hangs in the balance
We wait for the end

Isn't it a shame
This fascination
With death?

The death of the shell
While the spirit lingers?

Are we not part of the
Greater cult of personality
The court of the vulture?

Hank's Fourth

I had a strange dream last night
something about Jack Micheline
secretly frying bacon in the room where I was sleeping
"Jack"; I says
"Jack, you don't have to fry your bacon
in secret anymore 'cause you're dead..."
Jack looked at me in disbelief and sort of shimmered
like his vertical hold was going and he smiled that
toothless smile of his and winked out and vanished.

This morning I remembered that Monday
was the fourth anniversery of the death of Hank
I thought about how I'd celebrated his departure from this life:
I'd worked my ass off trying to finish a drywall job
Then a friend of mine came over and we made it
until eleven thirty p.m.
She thinks I'm sexy - I think
I'm too old to be sexy but if it works for her
who am I to ruin her vision.

It's a fitting tribute to the old man.

Have I Told You About the Rain?

It seems like it's always raining
Whether in my head or on it
Tonight it's doing both
But I have a roof over my head
I'm safe from fat drops
That are laying down
Across rooftops
A delicate patter that
Washes the sin away
The accumulated sin of
The innocent California sun
I watch the drips falling off the awning
As I stand on the landing
Listening to a pair of singers
Sultry plying their trade
On Austen City Limits

Tonight I think
It must be raining
All over the world

Have You Heard This One?

A winter sky smirks
On this chilly December night
I wonder what the joke is
This time?

2003 certainly had its moments:
I had a girlfriend who wanted sex
And nothing else and now
I have a girlfriend who wants
Everything else except the sex.

Is that the joke?

I owe the DMV a thousand bucks
For car registration on cars that
I don't even own anymore or
Can't drive because of needed repairs.

I got a fix-it ticket the other day
On my work van and now
The city of Long Beach
Wants $181 on top of the $352
The state wants to re-register it.

Is that the joke?

My landlord wants me out
But there's no place to move to yet
And I can't afford to go to
Maytag Heights because I'm
Not poor enough.

Is that the joke?

> > >

Both California and Long Beach
Are almost broke yet real estate
Is jumping off the map –
You can't rent a one bedroom
Apartment for under $700
Without living in a part of town
Where you're afraid to step outside.
Might as well live in your car.

Is that the joke?

Hiking the Rogue River Trail – 1972

for Karen Lang

I remember the images
Better than the story

Our failed trip to Toronto
Your aunt would have to wait
The bus ride back from
The Canadian border
Seattle in the rain
Hitchhiking thru Oregon
Getting stuck in Grant's Pass
A field of Mustard flowers
Some helpful hippies
Hiking 25 miles on an impulse
With my first love
The future still looking bright
Some water snakes peering over
The rocks at us in the cool
Of summer shade
Tromping mile after mile
Day after day
Happy as pigs in slop
In our hard labors
Toughing it and proudly so
Even as our plans to hike
To the coast were thwarted
The old truck that the ranger
Had resurrected giving us a lift
To pick up the road to the coast
Fresh picked Blackberry's on
Camp fire pancakes
And more friendly folk
A ride to the coast and then

> > >

All the way back to SanFran
Two hippies in a van with a
Box of cassettes and a shotgun
Bong with weed to share

Something reminded me of
Those mad yellow Mustard
Flowers this afternoon
A thin yellow mist floating
Over a field of green stems
Only visible as they undulated
In the wind

HIGHWIRE ACT

He gingerly steps out onto the high wire
Inching along the woven steel rope
A speck of crazy daredevil-may-care
Silhouetted against the sky full of
Blue indifference
A catch-your-breath-how-can-he-do-that?
And the daredevil thinks
Ah, the world is my oyster
It hangs in my balance
This moment is mine and mine alone
Watch me as I make my move
Will I succeed or will I perish?
He watches his feet
Feels the weight of the pole
The breath of wind in his hair
Observes birds in flight
And it is all so very
Frightening and wonderful

And yet

I sometimes think that we are
All inching out over an abyss
Even if it's of our own making
That we are at times
Instruments of crazy wonder and
Terror with our lives suspended
Over some improbability
And that the miracle of our success
Is as dubious as our being noticed
And acknowledged by those who
Can only afford the price of
Admission to the peanut gallery but
Who are wooed away from this
Daily spectacle of heroism by
A world that gleefully picks its
Winners and losers based on
Some crazy notion of who is
Important and who is mundane

Hospital Sequence

These hospital poems emerged from a two week stay at Memorial Hospital in 2013… It was my second two week stay in a hospital since I began my association with the Medicos.

In these poems I tried to capture the moods that washed over me. There was plenty of time to kill and there were plenty of memories that stuck in my mind. I meant to put these out as chapbook, but never got around to it. Eventually they just faded away.

Abandonment Issues

Going on 2 weeks now
Here in my room
The one constant through
This ordeal has been
The isolation and
Growing frustration
That nobody seems to be listening

The nurses chastise me
When I try to do things
On my own instead of
Asking for help but
When I ask for help
Nobody comes

The dietitian asks what I
Want to eat the following
Day but when the meals
Come they aren't what
I ordered anyway

It's very demoralizing

On top of it all the
Lonely hallways and
The fear of being lost
Within a system that
Manages hundreds of
Patients daily serves to
Wrap me in a
Blanket of fear

If ever there was a test of
My tenacity and self
Confidence then this might
Well be one of the top ten

Don't Lose Yo' Cool

While listening to Albert Collins
Sitting awkwardly in my hospital bed
My little white raft floating in my
Little world of "comfort"
I imagine the hospital staff jiving
And boogieing around my little raft
I can see Curtis* jumping to Albert's
Funky guitar riffs as he swings
One of the nurse's-aides in gay abandon

*one of the "transportation team" members

Dream Catcher

"I wander the outskirts
of sleep in a dawn
that reaches back
through dream fragments"

—From *"Trembling With My Angel"* by Rick Smith

Morning starts at 4 AM
I awake from a dream
Fumbling for my key
The old worn out one to
My 54 Chevy truck
More a suggestion than
Actual key
But in reality I am trying
To open the bedrail with
Part of my I.V.
Such are the delusions
Of a sleep-deprived
Nine toed man

I have begun to dream
Here in my fifth day
In a hospital in
Long Beach
Though my dreams are
Fragments of scenes
Glimpsed as if I am
Running parallel to them
Down a colonnade
Watching them flicker
On and off like an
Old time movie

> > >

In these dreams I am
Scared always being chased
By surly surgeons
Whipping their scalpels wildly
Back and forth
Trying to cut some more of me off

Haunted House

My new home is haunted

I hear the muffled voices
Inside the walls
And loud bangs and
Knocking as if an
Awful fight is going on

Sometimes I hear hysterical
Laughter and shrieking
Other times there are
Cries for help or retching

At night the lights go on
And off at will

This is life in Room 461

Hospital Codes

Here in the hospital
Most of the staff have
A dark sense of humor

I guess it's because they
See so much agony and
Injury that they must
Laugh it off or be dragged
Into the pit of despair that
Most of us patients
Call home

Once they see that I too
Have a wicked sense of humor
They sometimes open up
A little and give me a
Behind-the-scenes glimpse

The other day
Before I was due for another
Surgery on my foot
I expressed concern about
My on-again-off-again bouts
With diarrhea
Brought on by ten days of
Antibiotics and the doctor
Said calmly
Don't worry it won't be the
First time we've had to call
A Code Brown

Is there a Code Yellow I ask

Only if it's more than half a liter
The doc says without batting an eye

Ah! Hospital humor...

Hospital Diet

Gourmet hospital food?
Oxymoron
But I expect to get or
What I need
(Diabetics need a low-carb diet)
When I order
Given the choices
But after trying for
Twelve days to
Find a middle ground
With kitchen staff

I have given up on
The pretense of
"Ordering" my meals
In advance

They will send me
Whatever they want

And I will eat it
If I can

Morphine Dreaming

I tried not to cry,
Choking back tears,
I held your hand.
There wasn't much
Left to hold;
The cure and
The disease had
Made sure of that.
You lay motionless
In your bed,
As if you were
Waiting for a
Dark angel to
Draw your curtains shut;
As if each shallow
Breath could be
Your last.

It had been a long fight,
But I could see you were
Ready for it to end.
Was that fear I saw in your eyes
Or horror that you were
Still here,
In this mess
That only the living
Could cherish.

In the end,
You headed south,
While I remained here
Unable to move or speak

As another chapter in my life closed

Man's Burden

They dress you in a thin
Cotton gown open at the back
Plant you in a bed for 15 days
Surround you with women
Who wipe your ass when
You soil yourself and who
Tend to your ills and console
You when you are afraid
Laugh at your stupid jokes
And make you feel like
A human being when
Everything else around you
Makes you feel like a piece
Of meat and still you are
Expected to remain a non
Sexual being…

One night towards the end
Of my stay in room 461
I began to get horny
Really it had begun that
Afternoon during a visit
By one of the lovely
Women who came to
Pay their respects at
My bedside

I couldn't get her out
Of my head and by
Nightfall she had taken
Up residence like Poe's
Raven quoting "no way"
To my "go 'way" and
As the night slipped away

> > >

I found myself lost in
Fantasies of an oral nature

Somewhere after three a.m.
I awakened to the night nurse
Changing my I. V.
I must have dozed off
During my masturbation
Because my hand was still
Holding my penis

Thank god the nurse didn't
Turn on the light like every
Nurse had done before her
Or else I would have been
Exposed for the pervert
That everyone knows I am

I keep telling myself
That's not true
I'm not a pervert
Just a lonely old man

But the truth is
In today's world
That's exactly what
I am – a pervy old man.

Nocturnal Obsession

Unable to sleep
Because of thoughts
Of you
Half awake
Half asleep
Fantasizing about
Licking your muffin
Probing and nibbling
Hours spent
Lapping away

Lovely

Just not sure
The lack of sleep
Is worth the price
For this nocturnal
Obsession

Stir Crazy

It's been almost a month
Since I left Shirley and
Her sisters of mercy to
Come back here to this
Hovel this place cursed
With ghosts and strange
Creaking and groaning
I have been here for the whole
Time except for a few
Trips out for food and
Other necessities of
Life liberty and
The pursuit of
Happiness
But it
Isn't
Helping
Me much
I'm beginning
To hate where I hang
My hat these days this
Ramshackle place I used to
Think was funky and cool
With its peeling ceilings
Cracks in the walls and
Fading paint it's as they
Say in those old films from
The thirties about to drive
Me mad I've begun to hate
All the cracking and groaning
I can't stand it the same bed
The same scooter every time
I want to do anything beyond
My reach the same window
The same ceiling the same
BS with the HMO the same
Growing pain in my foot the same
Thing day in and day out

The Foot

I have to get more
work done on my foot,
or 'the foot' as the
medicos think of it.
'The foot' exists in
their universe, not
ours or even *mine*.
And every time
they cut into 'the foot'
their universe crunches
into my universe,
like a stop and go
Friday afternoon
on the 405.

Thankfully, their universe
only sideswipes mine,
most of the time;

no head-on's
so far.

The Loneliest Feeling

I can hear the world
Just beyond the curtain
It jostles and vibrates
With life, with laughter
The nurses chattering
Like monkeys in a tree
Alive with each day's activity
Each day's successes
Each day's failures

I can hear the world
Though it's but a
Microcosm of the
Actual world
The hustle and bustle
Of life like a river
That courses by me
While I stand on its
Banks unable to join in

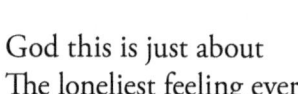

God this is just about
The loneliest feeling ever

On My Street

Day after day
This is my only
Connection to
The other world
The one on the other
Side of the glass
Cars creep by
Young adults ride
By on their bicycles
People walk by
Usually with a very
Small dog or two
Or I see just their heads
As they walk by my fence
Sometimes they are
Talking on their cell
Phones and stop and
Pace back and forth
Sharing their half of
The conversation with
Me and the birds and the
Squirrels who bound
Across the fence as if
It is their 405 freeway
At rush hour and in the
Morning little birds
Most likely sparrows
Clamor to sit on the
Same fence risking
A hit and run by
A tree squirrel as it
Makes its mad dash
Sometimes at night
I hear the shouts of

> > >

The inebriated coming
Home from some party
But mostly at night
It's just the sounds of
Cars and fire trucks
Going up and down
My street outside my window
Outside my life

Green Thumb

Remembering my landlady's words
"He has such a green thumb!"
I look over the ruins of my garden
Slowly dying from lack of water

It's nice to have a green thumb
But it doesn't do much good
If you can't reach the faucet

These days the
Simple act of
Washing a plate
Is all that's
Required to
Make it through

Dire Consequences

I admire her from afar
But I must use caution
It is written all over her
Not just because of
Her jealous boyfriend
Who can blame him
But because I am sure
She is like magnesium
Ready to burst into flame
Whenever it strikes her fancy
Or perhaps she is a gift-
Wrapped Medusa who can
Only be viewed in a mirror's
Reflection…

Ice Cubes & Black Coffee

Chewing on weighty issues of Sun & Moon
She breaks her teeth on ice cubes
"I can stand the pain"
she says
describing with stomach-churning detail
forty three hours under the drill
over the last two years
"I never take Novocaine or the gas.
The trick here is to drink your coffee
hot and black, preferably two or three days
beyond the normal limit
Stay up late
and always know where your moon is..."

Ignorance

It was summertime
and you promised that the living would be easy
that the fish would be jumpin' right onto our plates
already cooked
and we'd always be doing it in high cotton!

We thought you were rich
and mom was the best looking woman in the entire world
(except for Jackie-O and M. Monroe)
and you hushed us
and told us to keep our mouths shut

During the Summer of Love,
long before Jesus came back as a vato, ninja, corporate, terrorist, talk-show host,
I tripped out the door, saw a generation burning like Icarus
kissed the sky and fell at your feet
like another missed opportunity
as the camera pulled back for a wide shot
of America dreaming that the paint would never peel
and the picket fence would always stand tall and proud.

I hate

To be gross
But I turned
that chick
back to the
way of male
female relations
now she says
that what we had
was what she
needed for the
time?
Well I'm
Sorry to hear
That.
I'm sorry to
Hear that it
Wasn't mutual.

Mostly
I'm sorry to
Hear that what
We shared
Wasn't
Anything
Special
At all
No big deal
Just the swapping
Of fluids

Just garbage

Like I'm dead
Or something
Or nothing of
Importance

Just a stain

Shit

I Knew Your God

his name was Larry
I met him in an alley
off of Lime street
it was a cold night
there was a drizzle
and a light breeze
we were walking
when suddenly you
lurched behind a
dumpster grunting

when you emerged
your hair was wild
like grasses blown
before a storm and
your eyes were the
eyes of a madman

you wailed at me
flaying your arms
left and right and
moving towards
me like you were
some kind of crazy
thresher or some
thing menacing and
then you stopped
your head pointing
to the ground as if
you were ashamed
of something and
you looked up slow
ly when I said Bob
what's wrong? Bob?

and you said
Bob's not here
I'm Larry and
I'm going fuck
you up son I'm
gonna hurt you
unless you get
out of my sight
right now!

Larry started for me
I was scared – Bob
had told me about him
but this was the first
time I had met Larry
he was completely bat
shit nuts and out of
his ever-lovin' mind

as I turned to run away
he grabbed me by my
jacket collar and pulled
down hard
that's when the instinct
kicked in as I swung
around the knife appearing
in my hand as if by magic
swinging underhanded
into his gut and he fell
backwards screaming

there isn't much else
to say now except

> > >

Bob survived and
after being checked
out thoroughly by
the docs has been
declared completely
safe and sane like
a firework stand
no more Larry

now Bob sits alone
in a bar drinking
himself into
oblivion

I'm Tired

I am slowly dying of loneliness
The women no longer come to my door
Except when they need something
And the men only drop by to borrow money or tools
Or a slice of my own precious sanity
Success eludes my grasp
While the chaotic world continues to bestow
Riches and fame on fools and idiots
Everything is wearing out
Breaking down and
Generally turning to shit

And it occurs to me that
This is nothing newsworthy
Crap happens everywhere
People die of something everyday:
Lead poisoning
STDs
Heartbreak
Bad Junk
Bad pills
Bad attitude
Bad decisions
A myriad of medical conditions
On and on
It's heartbreaking

I am slowly dying of loneliness
Yet the Acacia blossoms are still a wonder to behold
And the purple light at dusk still highlights the houses along 8th Street
The Pabst Blue Ribbon still quenches a late afternoon thirst
My grim thoughts are still muted by an unexpected smile
Or kind word
And life isn't so bad
After all

Immortal Lines

Immortal lines of poetry
rising and falling
in the poet's mind
like lines of shiny, wet ink
that blur
immediately
upon contact with
the paper

reality is seldom
the hard slate that is required
seldom more than a roll of
toilet paper
hardly paper at all

scratching lines in the dirt
would be more profitable.

In the Shadow of the Jagged Moon

In this Eden of oddities
where the foliage is lush and
hides the cacti and Thorny Nettle. . .
In this Eden where I have lain
with you, contorting my
hulking shape to sleep
"like spoons" --
ladle and table spoon --
in moments of peace,
moments of sanctuary . . .
In this Eden of compromise
where tired dreams meet delusion
at the junction of Hope and Experience . . .
In this Eden where my whatevers
are your whenevers and no wind
blows no change and never will . . .
In this Eden of forbidden knowledge
where one approaches each bend
in the wood with an unnatural caution . . .
In this Eden where the apple,
at once the temple of knowledge
and at the same time, the
instrument of our downfall,
has begun to lose its magic over me . . .
In this Eden of deception
where my double life is no
longer the adventure it once was . . .
In this Eden where shadows
betray the hidden possibilities,
where the movement of time
can be glimpsed whenever the
jagged moon casts its ghostly
glow on the landscape . . .
In this Eden of miracles

> > >

where hiding inside my shadow
once seemed a small price to pay for
the nourishment of your company . . .
In this Eden where I would stay
wrapped in your arms until
the inconveniences disappeared,
where I would spend days willingly
were it not for the knowledge
that you couldn't or wouldn't
clear your calendar . . .

In this Eden of fixed variety
where the shadow of the Jagged Moon
dances across my conscience with
out concern and I can no longer keep pace.

Invisible on Aisle 5

The older I get
And the more
Banged up I get
The more I seem
To disappear

In the market
The other day
It seemed no one
Was aware of my
Presence at all
It was as if I had
Faded away in the
Canned vegetable
Section my jaunty
Flare unnoticed
By the elderly
Lady pushing
Her basket full
Of day-old's
And "manager's
Specials" she
Practically bump
Ed right into me
Or the man with
The worried look
On his face he
Hurriedly rushed
Head on into me
But he never touched me
As if I wasn't there
Anymore.

Yet it doesn't faze me   > > >

As if my condition
Might allow me a
Freedom to observe
My fellow man
Without hindrance
Noting the landscape
That seems to be no
Less than an Edward
Hopper panorama.

Note the two Mexicans
Observing the progress
Of the woman stopping
To light a cigarette
Dangling at a precarious
Angle from her lips
Or the line at the post
Office waiting to get on
With their day waiting
To get away from this
Hodgepodge of colors
Back to their own kind
Back to what's important.

Everywhere I go I'm
Aware that this Hopper-esque
World is overtaking my
Everyday life
There is no interaction
Between us so there is only
Disconnection and that
Gives Hopper the edge.

So I walk a fine line
Between connection and
Disconnection as long as I
Chat people up I am safe
But when I stop talking
I am free to observe and
Hopper takes over it's a
Great catch 22 – damned
If you do and damned if you don't
It's a helluva Vienna.

I Saw Yojimbo Today

After your words
I wanted to fall on
my sword, but in
the end, like the
dirty samurai, one
must square one's
shoulders and walk
off frame, alone.

Someone else will
have to roll 'credits'.

I thought I was

in trouble when
I couldn't seem
to write a poem
But then one
morning I woke up
and realized that
I couldn't keep it
up any more
And then the
poetry came!

It's My Own Fault

there's not much to say after that.
Everything sounds like a lame excuse
or some kinda plea.
some angles are better left alone
"Man did you see that angle?
Christ it was so obtuse,
it was flat!"

All you can do at times like these
is wave 'em off and
pray that they run outta fuel
before they get back again.

Ivy II

Ivy used to refer to her
Husband's dick as the
All American ten inch cock.
She didn't have much good
To say about it claimed it
Was gross and hard to take.
But now she regales me
With tales of her boyfriend's
Nine inch nail.
She loves his cock because
He doesn't care about hygiene;
Something that Ivy isn't too
Concerned about herself.
She used to fool around
With me but we never
Sealed the deal until years
Later and tho it was a one-off,
I wanted more.
But my five inch penis needs
An "apparatus" and Ivy needs
Four more inches and more
Time even tho I need more
Time too but maybe I need
More than she has patience for,
Plus I'm about four inches
Out of the big picture.
So maybe I'll just have to
Settle for a bottle of water
A keyhole and some K-Y…

Jacaranda

You work the same
sorry-assed job for all your life
living in the same rut
seeing the same faces
day in and day out
with the same stories
and the same
small talk
and the sameness
of the days collapse inwards
on your soul like
poorly kneaded bread dough
and everything is always the same
making you want to scream
from its familiarity
but you don't because
suddenly, smack-dab in the
middle of your rebellion
something unexpected has
planted itself.

Oh yes, the spring has come.

La Puerta Del Diablo

Estoy triste hoy
la luna sonríe como un gato
y me estoy hundiendo
como si estuviera atado con a stone
como si el diablo
ha abierto la puerta al infierno
y estoy siendo succionado
en el vortex

Qué latima
Tengo un palo, pero
no marshmallows!

Translation:

I am sad today
the moon is smiling like cat
and I am sinking
as if I am tied with a stone
as if the Devil
has opened the door to Hell
and I am being sucked
into the vortex

What a pity
I have a stick but
no marshmallows!

Leaf: Turning

I wait for you
like a leaf blowing at your feet
swirling across your path

a leaf of no distinguishing
feature, an unexceptional
leaf, just a green shape
turning yellow
blowing through on my
way on to somewhere else

yet you are there
with your feet shuffling
down this path
unsuspecting
that we will cross
each other

that our journeys
could ever intersect

what are the odds
what are the chances
that you and I would
meet in this way

in my youth when I was
still hanging from the tree
you might have admired
the leafy community
that I called home
hanging there in space
with my fellow leaves

it was a season of light
and dark, of sun and shade
of movement
and stillness

now I am blown into your
path, drawn by fate or
some other magnetism
to this junction
as if you called me
and I had no recourse
but to come.

Life On The Street

October
11 years back
the BIG adventure
evicted for indecent behavior
Read Huckleberry Finn for inspiration
by flashlight
Homemade camper
moved from town to town
up and down the southern coast
Relied heavily on the kindnesses of
strangers
Lived out of an ice chest
Cooked on a camp stove
Saw many a sunrise through blood-shot eyes
Seemed to be quite happy to be living
foot-loose and fancy free
Wasn't
Longed for a bathroom with a door
Dreamed of a home that didn't rock in the wind
a home that stayed in one spot
a fixed spot in the universe to return to
my spot.
Envied those with a place
who
in turn
envied me and my "freedom"
Drank myself to sleep 'most every night
Felt abandoned and lost
Made the best of it
Kept coming around
like some ghost
haunting the places where
I once "lived"

Could feel life draining out of me
like a bathtub suicide
nearly made it
but didn't have the guts
The joyous life of the Gypsy (homeless)
and the mystique of the road
I know the real truth about these things
It takes real guts to survive a
life on the street and not get lost in the process

Lonely Girl

Mocked by crows
The pale-skinned girl
Wanders the streets
Under gray skies
Her inky black attire
As perfect as a pebble
Underwater

Winter approaches
A time of drawing in

The pale-skinned girl
Longs for a cool embrace
To take her beyond
The realm of this exquisite pain
Beyond
This clearing
Where the gleaming
Of her black pebble
Catches the eye
Of her tormentor

Her blood betrays
The burning rush of desire

In the end
The rustle of branches
Punctuated with cawing
As smoke lays down
And blankets the ground

Smelling like the first cigarette

Lucid Thought #2

It's funny
how things fall
into place,
as if a flurry
of unseen
hands were
constantly
adjusting
the strings
that determine
our every action.

While we
struggle to
find our way
as if we have
any say in
the control
of our lives.

Maybe that's
really the
origin of
the wind:
a game of
patty-cake
between
Fate and Destiny.

Maturity

"Have you seen him lately!?"
She queries
Yeah, I say,
with his dye job tied in back
like an art fag ponytail;
his tight jeans and leather jacket
the zippers all magnificently chromed
as if the whole thing is preserved in a sealed vault
after each outing,
like Michael Jackson,
a sleeping beauty in a cryogenic chamber.
I'd fuck him myself if it weren't
for the repercussions,
I say
"You're sick" she chortles
As I recall it,
you did, on a regular basis
so, who's the sicker?
"Yeah. I don't know what I ever saw in that guy
I musta been lonely and desperate
Thank God I've moved on"
Yes, thank God
by the way, when's your boyfriend due for release?
"Next May"
she replies.

Memorial Day

I once wrote that the poem would save you
but it ain't gonna save me this a.m.
as I get ready to go to work
while everyone else, well
almost everyone else, gets ready to
honor the dead by the sacred ritual
of the burning of the flesh
either on the grill
or on the dirty sands
that border the oceans.

But it's just another day
for the self-employed
just another job
in another town.

The jobs are most always
the same type
for them you need a head
a pair of hands
and a strong back
(good legs don't hurt either)
only the locales change
dramatically.

This day
I'm off to complete
a painting job that
I"ve been working on for two
plus weeks, over in Redondo Beach
It's pleasant enough work
though the owner is sour
most of the time
but he's just finished a career in   > > >

engineering and I'm sure
that dealing with the human race
is not as easy as the race of numbers
Humans are predictable
within a certain degree of variables
but numbers are always consistent
and do what they set out to do
So I'm sure that "we" are a big
disappointment.

His resignation is obvious
it's hopeless
he's in "our" world now
nothing can be done
about that.

Nothing but finish the job
and move on.

Missing You

After four days of being with you
I return to my apartment, which
I notice smells like a freshly dug grave.

I find myself missing
you on a biological level

Your body has made an imprint on me
My bed seems a foreign place
and someone has made my pillows
into a pile of stones. This is
not my bed, I think, and
you are not my lover, I say
to the black and white panda bear,
my bed-mate through those
lonely years before I met you.

"What have you done with her,
you bastard! Where is she?" I want to
scream at the face in the mirror.

I can't wait for the weekend to come
again so I can rush back into your arms,
into your sweet, sweet arms. Your love
fills my head with a crazy desire
but I must "suck it up" and get ready for
another day of work.

My Head is a Soggy Sponge Full of Other People's Dreams

the editor's poem

I'm typing some of the best poetry I've done in years
Unfortunately, 75% of it is someone else's
I see red, but it is someone else's complication
There are unexploded mines littering
the floor of my apartment, but
they were left behind by Bill Shields
on his way to meet Buk and Dos for lunch
I have become the Sorcerer's Apprentice
. . .the buckets of slop keep coming
and I can't remember
how to
reverse
the spell
and end
this charade.

New Year's Eve 2003

A small cup of brandy
Warming on the heater
Oatmeal heats up as well
Two swigs of grapefruit juice
I pull on white socks
One with a hole in the heel
New blood stains on my jeans
From glass slivers yesterday
- Tile job from hell -
Coffee awaits me down the street
Rent paid for another month
Bills still due
Car tags still unpaid
Hope: growing thin
Love: unlikely throbbing
Pain: dull murderous constant
Resignation: pending notification
Debt: unrelenting tide
Life: I'm a little boy barely able
To see past the crowd as the
Parade flashes by
Oatmeal is hot and thick now
Soon I'll be at work
Spastic words of hate
Echoing in my brain
Waiting for them to die out
Waiting for the music to start
Waiting for the next phase to begin

No Excuse For Domestic Violence

There it was
plainly written
on the rear bumper of the
black and white.
So what did this mean?
Was it okay to beat
your fellow worker?
Was it okay to beat
your average foreigner?
That any kind of violence is permissible
in our modern
civilized world
is a concept that I don't
grasp.

Number 7

You came
mouth open
breathing deeply
as I moved
inside you
slowly

No mountain tumbled
to the sea
no worlds exploded
no great wind
rushed up and
swept you away

Yet you came
mouth as open
as my heart
as much as I
wanted you
you came

And afterwards
for the first time
you didn't run away.

Obligation

I'm going to a poetry reading
I'd rather be doing other things
like the laundry
or the grocery shopping
or just driving around the hill
or making a few calls
or pricing lumber
or sucking up a cold one
or even watching the tube

Instead
I'm going to a poetry reading AND art reception
for all I know it will be a room full of man-haters
and art fags
so
in order
to set the mood
I'm going to read some Bukowski
and hope that the luck holds

Odysseus Returned

from the sea
a wiser man
a humbled man
returned to his queen
who waited
a prisoner within
the walls of her home
and her promise of fidelity.

She wove a tapestry
each thread a sigh,
a telling note from her heart,
each day she wove
and each night she
unraveled it.

Now, I am no Penelope
and you, no Odysseus
but when you finally return
to me and I tell you how each
day I wove a tale
and each night, oh how
I unraveled it...

you better believe me.

You better believe how I
pined away, waiting for
the wind to bring you home
with arms spread wide
like a ship running before the wind
How I've longed for your embrace.

Answer my prayers:
honor me
hurry your voyage home.

On Growing Old

A lesson from the vegetable garden

Growing old the
Vegetable produces
Flowers and seeds
Before death turns
It to back into mulch
To fertilize the next
Generation.
How silly are we to presume
That growing old is something
To avoid as if our cycles are
Any different than the natural
Order of things
As if we are so special or
So different than other life forms
Here on this little blue ball
We call home.

On Returning Home

The gravity of the familiar
The Blending of memory & fact
The slow parade of mourners
The lost brother
A blizzard of paper snow
The pilgrimage accomplished
The familiar landscape
The smile of recognition
The prodigal son
The tragic Oedipus
The reluctant gypsy
Orpheus the adventurer
Jason on the horizon
Brave Richard at the Channel

Kindred spirits all
Yearning for reunion
and a respite from
the heat of battle.

On The Death Of Mike Adams

His poetry could be
As brisk as the air on any
Mountain meadow or as
Sweet as a good woman's smile

He was a kind and
Generous man whom
Rumor has it never
Got mad but he was
Also the kind of man
That you knew you didn't
Want to fuck with

Even death knew this
Death had to come at
Him sideways when
He wasn't lookin'
Death can be chicken
Shit like that

But even a cheap
Shot like that
Can't diminish
What Mike
Meant

He was a real human
Being and a good one
At that and now
That he's gone
It will take at least
Five good men to
Carry-on where
He has left off

On the Margin

Revised

A loose mirror on the passenger side
A leaky seal
A failing wheel cylinder
A bald tire
A wet oily street
A broken camera lens
Bad tubes
Dull blades
Unpaid debts
Broken dreams
No hot water
Stains on the sheets
A weed choked garden
A hair choked drain
A strange hand in your pocket
A finger on the trigger
A pain in the ass
Blood in the toilet
The wrong time to turn over a new leaf
A broken rubber
A broken heart
An insensitive remark
A sideways glance
A caution thrown to the wind
A dirty secret
Boredom
Four walls closing in fast
A few steps from insanity
A few more steps from a cardboard box under a bridge
A misstep
A knock at the door
A broken shoelace

It's not the big issues that take you down
It's the little moments that ambush you
A broken pencil
A hard drive crashing taking all of your poems

One Finger At A Time

Flipped off by a carload of
young anglo boys
while avoiding an unannounced
right hand turn
swerving into the left lane
coming down Gaffey hill at 22nd Street

Their anger
burning like dripping steel under
the welder's torch
lasted all the way
to 9th Street where they let up
and headed off towards L.A.
and some other brand of trouble.

I've been in this bind before
but learning my lesson then
did not push this one
farther than it needed
to go.

Driving has become as easy as
dancing in a minefield.

One For The Road

Years relegated to the slow lane
spent in old vehicles
old cars
old trucks
older by a decade than myself
older by more than a decade
than the very asphalt that we speed over
day and night
week after week
Years spent cruisin' in the right lane
because the speed limit would not allow
the old rustbucket to cut in line.
Twenty years ago
the silver lining on the gas crisis
was a double nickel miracle
Suddenly
the old wreck is able to join the parade
Suddenly
I am able to pass on the left!

Now tragedy repeats
even though it is I who is now the older
and the cars are a mere
twenty or thirty years old
and I am upwardly mobile
all that changes this week.
Gone is the feeling of comradery
of membership in a special club
Lost again in a cloud of blue smoke
as the pack accelerates
legally
to sixty five and beyond
and while speedsters dream of moving to Montana
where they can roar past the millennium   > > >

and not worry about a speed trap
I long for those days now gone
when the sight of the old geezer
in the old rustbucket
inspired awe in the hearts of some
and terror in hearts of many
as we thundered past
tool box a'rattling
going FIVE MILES OVER the speed limit!

Now I'm back in the right lane
all too familiar territory
and here I'll stay
because the chances of my ever owning
anything that moves fast enough
to pass on the left again lays
somewhere between Winslow and Kingman
along Route Sixty Six.

Outside the Zen Center

Cool night breath
opens jasmine blossom
with the certainty of a
lovers caress
as sweet as a
parting kiss

poem

The broken bones smile
rust spots on the carpet and
melons rot in the darkness
unseen
index finger taps
out solitude's elusive
s.o.s.

Portrait

The photographer said
"I want you to just be yourself
no airs"
He assured me that he
wanted a photo that,
like me,
put on no pretense
no posturing
just a straight-ahead view.
When it was done
he called me to say it was on the way.
I picked up the envelope from
the General Delivery
and eagerly opened it
It was harsh
uncompromising
no-holds-barred
I looked at the camera
not with disgust
or anger
neither aloof
nor smug
Can this be what
others see when they look
in my direction?
I am neither handsome
nor ugly
merely rough
like a stucco wall
or sandstone cliff
Is this the face
that sees the brutality
woven through the beauty
of this tapestry?   > > >

Is this what has
become of the face
that yearned for the caress
of the lover's hand?
That sought pale shelter
in love's sweet arms?
This is not a face burned down
by life's vigorous flame
but merely worn away
eroded by imaginary tears
disappearing under the
unrelenting hands of time.

Rain coming down

And I'm thinking
Of you
But it's a universal you
A you that incorporates
All the actual you's
That I have known
And the idealized you's
Because I am here
Now
And I am here
Now alone
And yet
Somehow
In my aloneness
I think that there is
A you
Waiting out there
For me.
Possibly even
Looking for me

So stupidly
I wait
Here
In this
Splashing wilderness
The rain coming
Down
And
Me waiting
Looking for a
Sign
In the
Wilderness

Reality Check

There is a point
Where the concept of
Old
Is surpassed by
The reality of
Old
When you notice that
Things you vaguely
Worried about yesterday
Are no longer tomorrow's
Burdens but have become
Today's realities

Those little aches and pains
Now blossoming into
Conditions
Conditions that will not
Be easily overcome or
May never be overcome
The little warning signs
That you are beginning to
Fall apart – that your days
Are truly numbered

And as the knowledge that
These debilitation's that you've seen
In others are fast becoming your own
You marvel at your own naivete:
Thinking you'll just work until you die
Forgetting that you may not be able to
Pick up a hammer or hold a paint brush
Long before time's indiscriminate
Attrition takes its final toll on you

Requiem For A Jazz Drummer

She crosses herself at the casket's edge
As we look down into eternities silence.
Death is not as peaceful as we were told it would be.
Not merely an ending, it's also bad makeup and
An out-of-context repose
Hands that look like extra large flesh gloves
Covering hands that were once delicate
A timekeepers hands, holding a perfect rose
Instead of drumsticks or brushes.
Hands that kept perfect time once
Now monstrous and out of time
Forever.

I knew this guy named Mike Indovina
He was an average guy with the usual set of problems that are common
To these times we live in: marriage, then divorce, unusual living situations.
He had some kids, some jobs, some habits (good and bad)
Nothing really out of the ordinary except for this one gift:
Mike was an excellent drummer.
He had a sweet feel for rhythm and syncopation, watching
Him play, you could tell he was born to the task.
What he may have lacked in the other parts of his life
He made up for in his craft as a musician.
The man had finesse, a quality that can make or break a song.
His timing was impeccable, his knowledge of jazz (his chosen
Genre) seemed unlimited, and his gift brought the "straight ahead" stuff
To a broad audience over the years.

I don't know much about Mike's life outside the arena of music
But in the twelve years or so that have passed since I first heard him
In the Toth-Indovina Quintet, he never ceased to amaze me.
He was always sneaking in some tasty lick or clowning behind a soloist
In an otherwise serious moment.
Perhaps Mike was most alive when he was behind his kit, the troubles

> > >

Of the world being blown off the bandstand by a Ralph Gibson solo.
Music has a way of bringing out the best we have to offer and
Jazz has its own unique magic that enhances this when all the
Players are in the "pocket".
I'd have to say that Mike was in his element when he played with
Paul Toth (bass) and Ralph G (sax) and, in later years, Jim Fisk (guitar).
Some of my best memories are of Sunday afternoons in San Pedro
Working at Sacred Grounds Coffeehouse while Paul and Ralph and
Mike grooved down Green Dolphin Street.

There is a saying that a person dies twice: once, at the time of their
Actual death, and once, when the last person they touched forgets them.
I'd like to think that Mike will live for a very long time.

So, Mike, this one's for you buddy –
(I'm humming Green Dolphin Street in my head seeing your smiling face as I do)

Red State Blues

Random thoughts
After the election

The laces on my boots
Resemble black hair
Thick and long
Floating under water

I wonder which will
Go up sooner
The murder rate or
Suicide

Is that heart burn
Or is my left arm
Really going numb

Should I stay just
So I can have a good
Story to tell the gals
At senior bingo

Or should I go
And watch the
Carnage from
A different
Perspective

Resistance

while driving I often
put my hand out the
window and "fly"

my hand pushes against
the wind and at sixty
it almost feels like
I'm caressing your face
or your breast or shoulder
or any round place big enough
to get my hand around
but when the car slows down
my hand drops and the only
thing I can caress is
the dirty hot metal of
the car roof

my hand hungers for
your cool round places
but there is precious
little wind in this
long hot summer
and nothing of
consequence to push against

Road Rage

Last month on a trip
To San Diego the five freeway
Was closed trapping fifteen
miles worth of bumper to bumper
traffic between Oceanside
and San Clemente.

A bank robbery suspect was
Holding himself hostage and
Fearing a shootout the police shut
Down the five for two hours.

As my neighbors all around me
Contemplated justifiable
homicide I notice
A sign on the back of a tour
Bus ahead of me: San Diego
Half the fun is getting there.

Turkey vultures circle aimlessly
Overhead in a big pale blue sky
Steel and glass sparkle under
The summer sun baking the
Frustrated people who race
back and forth like so many
self-important ants on an
asphalt hot-plate.

There is nothing to do but
Wait it out no place to go
Nothing but irony to read
No one is smiling but the
Swat sharp shooter and
Those damn vultures.

Sad and Lonesome Blues

I'm so sad and lonesome
I'm beyond crying.
When I try to squeeze
out a tear or two
I only get dust.
I'm so sad and lonesome,
wolves come to me
to howl for them.
I'm so sad and lonesome
poets become giddy
in my presence.
I'm so sad and lonesome
grieving mothers from
around the world
turn to me for solace.
I'm so sad and lonesome
birds stop singing
whenever they fly
over my house and
the sun doesn't shine
on my garden any more.
I'm so sad and lonesome
fruit in the trees
wither and drop
as I walk by.
I'm so sad and lonesome
even crab grass dies
under foot as I cross
the neighbor's lawn.
Why am I so sad and lonesome?
Because no one comes
around to see me and
since no one comes around
I get even sadder and
more lonesome and

that's how sad and lonesome I am.
Even old Hank W. was never
that lonesome or that sad.

Santa Ana

At dusk
All the colors
Are muted

The trees lazily
Swing their
Branches like
Tired children
Returning home
For dinner

The air is cool
Refreshing
With no hint
Of tomorrow's
Heat

For now it
Seems as
Though most
Of the
World is
Honoring the
Cease-fire

Sitting in my bed

sandpaper head
scraping bits of paint
from dilapidated walls
bits that lay on pillows
waiting to brushed off
like annoying flakes of
plaster dandruff.
Sitting in my bed
the rain pulsing
outside my window
bringing winter's fresh
sweetness of chill and damp
to my darkened sanctuary
Sitting in my bed
reading the gospel
according to Tracey Lee
and Pleasant Gee
my cock rising and falling
like an aroused barometer
waiting for the release
waiting to drool like an idiot
and spit its lovin' spoonful
onto dispassionate sheets
Sitting in my bed
dreaming of a thousand kisses
past stroking past ghost
memories like a gallery of faces
along the sidelines
accelerating as the finish line
comes into view
Sitting in my bed
damaged goods
my only companion
my always-true-love

coming to no good
the day beginning and me
already spent and climbing
out of my shallow grave
one more time to face
the sunrise like Lorca
faced the firing squad with
Sad eyes and a sardonic grin.

Slice Of Life

With a cool precision
fate delivers another blow
to the body

Last time it was from a stranger
this time
a friend

you stand in the sunlight
staring at the ground
where a piece of you
lays dying
one more slice
of your life
gone

Something that My Dream Mother said

You are your father's son
you can't expect much
so
don't
and you won't be disappointed

How can I argue
with such wisdom?

She wanted my happiness
and taught me how to
live on scraps
as if she had seen what the future
would bring
as if it had been revealed
in dream-time
foretold in prophecy:
Expect little
and you won't be disappointed.

And I wasn't

Something's Wrong Here

A woman
neatly dressed
in clean clothes
with a set of
headphones on
her Afro-American
head and some
nice looking
rings on her
tiny little fingers
steps up to the
counter at the
bookstore &
asks me to
buy her some
food.

There's something
terribly wrong here.

Every article of
clothing that I'm
wearing has a hole
in it, and it's not a
fashion statement
My pants are more
thread-bare than
thread in certain
key places and
everything I own
is old or used or
hand-me-down
and every dime
that I have I had

to scramble for
doing little bull-
shit jobs, cutting
corners, scrimping
and saving just to
tread water, just to
eke out a subsistence.

She probably has more
money on her right now
than I do and SHE asks
ME to buy her food?!

There's something really screwed up with this picture.

I think of those who are already gathering dust and I wonder about them
I picture their faces, their bodies laid out in the final contentment
eyes closed and serenely drifting off to Valhalla
(or so we're told)
Maybe it's that March ninth
looms tomorrow
the date that Mr. Bukowski, leaned over and
penetrated the other side
reminding me each year that I'm that much closer to the same fate
the only fate that we all share in common with everything
ashes to ashes
dust to dust
all things will end
and, perhaps, good riddance, who knows? Not me, that's for sure
And all this while Saturday March eighth rolls along

um, so
uh...   > > >

shadow of a bird passes over awning
and the world's biggest cat draws another comment
and this is it

Me, the books, the parade, the cat, the awning, the day
oh yeah, this is definitely it!

SOS

I ran into one of my old girlfriends
at the corner table
where the whole mess began
She looked fine!
As usual
So of course I got ideas
Not because I still carry a torch
or anything like that for her
I just missed her lips
and her warm youth
spreading around me
like the laughing sun
on a warm, summer's day
But the present is never like the past
and what I got was sarcasm
and accusations
an unrelenting litany of "I know's"
and "You did's"
No kiss or gentle loving
in sight

Spell Breaker

Standing outside of Sam's Book City
in N. Hollywood the other night
talking to Tracy, the editor/publisher
of a small press magazine called,
"Damaged Goods" while attending
a reading featuring, among others,
Jack Michelene - the last of the
living beats / except for LF & Gary
Snyder (the forgotten beat), when
we are joined by the poet Doc Moss
(a likable guy) and continue to
discuss the pros and cons of life vs art,
whatever, it doesn't really matter at all
as long as the talking keeps her nearby;
but eventually she wanders off to get
a coffee and I look at Doc and say,
"That's why I'm into poetry... for the chicks!"
He laughs, because he knows as
well as I do that you get more poetry
from women, than you get women
from poetry. That is the one constant
that you can count on, always.

STONE

It's another gray summers day
muggy and warm
birds chirping outside
the neighborhood unusually still
an oscillating fan whispers into my ear
Rex, the wonder dog ,barks
at nothing, as usual
and I sit here, waiting
listening to Eric Satie.

Gray mood music
for gray matter.

Here, in Pedro, someone is very close to death
I can sense it
It's not just the music
or the day.
Everywhere, all around me
the sense of sadness, of grieving
always the weary, woebegone faces
sad-eyed and heart-broken
longing for that eternal rest
that big sleep.
And me?
Longing for that incantation
that will end this suffering
the spell to break free from
this damn weight
this crushing stone of a life.

Stop

Sometimes
After a long drought
I have to throttle the words
out of my mind
in order to make them work right
in order to shake them loose
in order to shake them out
onto the page
to form something
that might make some sense
sometimes it doesn't work out –
like now.

Then I'm left with
a vague feeling of disgust
of self-hatred,
of fear
that it has finally happened and
I can't make the words
do cartwheels anymore
and I must now sit and wait for
them to come to life
and show me the way.

It could be a long wait.

Strange in October

A strangely familiar wind
Is blowing in from the east
From where the pachucos
Migrated during the meth wars
Their labs built and populated
The Corona Hills
They have since returned to
The desert to Morongo or
Lancaster and points east
Leaving this land of hot
Dry winds that blow
Strange in October

Street Zendo and Drunken Koans

Hot and smoggy / smoke clouds my eyes / my mind/ my body / my mine / eeeny meeney mo / minney / minute / minuet / minue / minudo // hand slaps meat / slaps flesh / slaps cheek / slaps face / slaps hand / slaps air / slaps nothing // 01 = 50 years old / is it just a dream? // there's a red button with my name on it / war hysteria / the frantic pace / draws us towards a final solution / we secretly long for it / no more worries / no more sorrows / hoping for a masterful hand to save us / from ourselves / fry us if you must / but save us / we act as if we can't stop ourselves / can't be contained / or controlled / as if only the higher power can save us / lead us like lambs to slaughter / or salvation / ascending / or descending / the luck of the draw / starting in sin / working our way up the ladder / buying the myth / on time / hoping for a good return on the investment // the weather cools again / pre-birthday blues / I notice the horizon line / beyond the ozone line / a tiny / tumbling / light / unconnected from the rest of the tiny lights / a lone microbe / in the cosmic flood / dancing particles / ephemera from big bang / bits of starry sky // ...am I really here? / cdl # XXXX / SSN XXXX dash something something / checking account # XXXX / I make money / I spend it / money defines me / if there's no money / do I become invisible? // my heart is an abandoned warehouse / littered with junk / begging to be explored / a sense of danger / the air charged with foreboding / as if the shadow knows / but won't tell / as if to say / caution / danger / something to be reckoned with / waiting / bidding time / calculating my strengths / my weaknesses / assessing my actions / waiting for a clean shot //

Table Scraps

Was it a misunderstanding?
A light breeze moves the curtain
in an afternoon memory
a long forgotten dream that rises and falls
an image of breathing, spoken to a lover
as our own breaths,
in silent metaphor for our innocence,
were woven together, twining
like two vines in tandem,
growing into and around each other.
I pause and study my hand:
it's ruddy skin and shiny callouses,
dinged and dented by manual labor.
I trace the outline of the scar
on my thumb, a trophy of some adventure
forty years ago.
I return to my mother,
in her own gentle way,
telling me not to expect much out of life.
Did I misunderstand her?
Thinking she wanted me to learn to live on table scraps,
like some farm dog,
to grow up tough and proud
never needing to rely on anyone for anything.
I think of how much like a little boy I am now,
how much I need right now,
how much I need to be scooped up and held.

A light breeze like a quiet breath
plays with the hem of the curtain.
My hands begin to look old.
I wonder what miracle I will pull
from this junk pile
next?

Tarnished Crown

He sits in the corner
hunched in a chair
poised
like a sprinter
waiting for the gun
He is lord and master of this corner
this pile of papers
this TV
ashtrays filled to the brim.
Chain-smoking
he looks up at me and remarks
"No matter how much I try
to change
I always end up with
shit!"
Maybe you should try
working with a different
material
I think to myself.
Weeks go by
When I see him again
I know that something's changed
between us
The ease is gone
I was fortunate enough to be
invited into the inner circle
but I blew it.
It's not an easy stroll
back down the aisle
resigning from his court.

Tears Have No Color

– something I heard on the radio after 9-11

everyone grieves

from Hitler's kin
to those of Jesus Christ
from the suicide bomber's folks
to Reagan's minions
to the Raylettes
despite who's in power
to who is not
death
brings all hearts to one cause
one moment of insufferable loss

tears do not know ideology
nor philosophy
nor dogma
nor borders
nor race or creed

no matter how bad
or good you were
inevitably someone will shed
tears in your memory
and whether it's right or wrong
those tears will be heartfelt
will be real
not just a made for TV moment
whether you were a sombitch from
this side of the tracks or t'other
some one will mourn your loss
will feel that pang
when thinking of calling you

> > >

knowing
after a few heartbeats
that you will not pick up
knowing the emptiness
that follows will not
easily go
away

Thanks

I was watching The Tube
It was Thanksgiving
and I was watching various
parades and whatnot
It was during the segment on
The Ice Dance
that I thought:
"People sure go thru a lot of trouble
just to recreate a
beautiful moment!"
And I began to think about
all the beautiful moments in my life
in just the past year
the past month
the past days

A look
a touch
a light in your eyes
in your hair
a word, murmured
a clever turn of a phrase
the petal of a yellow flower
caught in the sunlight
nearly-transparent
the morning breeze
in the leaves
of the banana trees
right now as I write this
the blending of the music
and the birds
and the clicks of my fingers
on the keys

> > >

And the sight of this poem
unfolding
before me.

So this is what I give thanks for
to still remember how to see
the beauty
of each moment
and remember it

The Beast

It's inevitable
each day, sometime
during it I will
live with the beast

I will have to confront
the damned thing
in some dank hallway
in the ruined flophouse of memory
or run from it
naked and afraid
into nightmare suites
or hide, breathless
as it passes close by
or watch it from the safety
of some intellectual tree-top
as it hunts for me far below.

The Beast

It prowls the abandoned buildings and
claws it's way through the grim alleys
where derelicts are all that remain
of ill-conceived dreams of glory;
never acted upon
never enough faith to initiate.

The Beast

Give me a whip
and a chair, that I may
address you, you god-damned
trouble-maker!

The Bukowski Tour

Recent developments in the unfolding
mythology of the writer Charles Bukowski
have led me to create the "Ordinary Tales of Madness, San Pedro's Eccentric Writer's Tour."
SPEW for short
More affectionately know as the 'Hank' Tour.
Employees of the Hank Tour will all wear
the Hank uniform - Khaki slacks, a button-down shirt, casual (plaid pattern),
Sandals and Straw Fedora; they will smoke
Beedies and drink red wine
and they will each wear a button with a picture
of the old dog and the words: "Ask
me about Bukowski!" scrawled across the bottom
in jaunty, red letters.
Employees must be knowledgeable in the lore
of Hank, or must be good bullshitters (preferably both).
A knowledge of French and German is advisable.
The tour will include the grave site, a drive down
his street, a tour of the bars in Pedro that he never went to,
lunch at Zen-Fu-Ku, dinner at Nam's Red Door,
and a trip to the Post Office
(where the Wino's still sing his praises).
For an extra charge
a trip to Hollywood Park can be thrown in
but this will cost you, dearly.
Expect questions like:
"What was his favorite drink?"
"What did he die of?"
"Which house did he live in?"
"Was he better than Ginsberg?"
"Was he as good as Kerouac?"
"How often did he beat-up his wife?"
"Did you ever get drunk with him?"
"Were you a friend of his?"
"How long did you know him?"

"Is it true that he never did any of the stuff he wrote about?"
"Did he like to fuck young girls?"
"Was he really gay?"
"Are you a poet?"
"Was he really that depressed?"
"Was he a fake?"
"Why was he so famous?"
"Do you miss him?"
"Was he better than the 'East Coast' poets?"
Employees will be expected to further the myth
by embellishing wildly on the answers to these,
and other, questions.
Remember the company motto:
Don't Try

The Curse

The bubbling, giggling, chattering gaiety of
women
at the table next to mine casts a pall over my
otherwise comfortably cozy dim morning coffee.

Taking a break from this tedium
I eavesdrop on them
circling them in my mind's eye
like a camera recording a scratchy
black and white film in the style
of cinema verite, I notice first
the intricate ballet of their arms,
hands and legs,
then smiling mouths and eyes,
the placement of cups,
relative to hands, on the table,
cigarettes appear with a flourish
lips wrapping around filter-tips
forming little "O's" of pleasure
around little sticks of death.

I pause here to think about
how these women, whom I
know, enjoy sucking on things
that give them pain under the
guise of pleasure.

Then it's off to run the errands and
do the housework and tend to the
children and the boyfriends and
the husbands and so on.
And I return to this, to this
tedium, with the memory
of their nervous chatter fading
under the clattering of their keys.

The Doormat's Revenge

Before you know it, You're old enough to know better, but young enough to still not know why.

I've stood in the doorway and watched the ass-end of life walk away from me more times than I care to admit, much less recall. Thinking back on it now, it seems to me that the days that led up to this moment, this illumination, those moments of reckless abandon and questionable judgment have led me to the spot where I am now rooted. I pace back and forth or nervously move from one foot to the other, fretting like a "football widow" waiting impatiently for the season's end. I wait like a loyal dog, stupid with yearning and hunger for the master's return.

My biggest mistake was in ever admitting the dependence on all of the "you's", on all the members of the human race or even upon the affections of the animal world. Owning up to my allegiance to the universe or some cosmology of a like nature was, perhaps, my second.

But, thanks to some simple household ingredients and a clever device that I constructed from plans that I pulled off the Internet, I'm happy to report that the trap is laid. I'm waiting for your return.

Go ahead. Step on me.

The Eye Moves On

One
gets the
impression
that we
have
been
living
in the
eye
of the
storm
for the
past
eight
years.

Now
I
don't
know
if the
next
four
years
will
be as
destructive
as that
eye
moves
on to
another
location,
but I
do know
that some
of us
will be
tested.

The Flower

A flower once bloomed
Over this shit pile
It smiled
If flowers can
And radiated its
Magic for a while
And I do miss
It so

And even though
It's been years
So many years
So long that
Perhaps my memories
Are tinged by a
Wishful nostalgia
That colors the
Images of that time
I am still in love
With that flower
And that time
When she
Blessed my shit
Pile with her
Radiance

The fine print

the emergency room was
nearly empty and there
were only a couple of
ne'er do wells in line
ahead of me

thinking my luck had
changed I dreamed of
early release

my best time so far
had been five hours
the worst twenty-eight

I sat down on my bed
in my cubicle and waited
for the doc

I noticed a shuffling sound
as if a wind was picking up
but how could this be
I wasn't outside

and then I realized it was
the sound of dozens of
feet shuffling quickly into
the examination area
soon there were doctors
nurses and scared mothers
flooding into this room

through the curtain walls
I heard voices of comfort
voices of confusion and fear

voices of dazed children
uh oh there goes my
speedy exit

I had arrived about thirty
minutes ahead of the victims
of a school bus crash

children come first
they are the future
and I'm headed for
the pasture

Oh boy! I'm fucked

The Junk Man

"Don't slip / the anomalies are pure / the sky is red / the raindrops are loaded / with the eyes of children"
—From <u>Blood on the Floor</u>, by Normal

the junk man takes
his junk out
of his pants
and plays with it
but it is all rubbery
and messed up
like a Spanish painter
with nightmares
of Guernica.

The junk man
listens to the
sad stories
and waits for
a bird to sing him
to sleep but among
the fog no one can
fly and the
singing wires
refute the tune.

The junk man takes
out his junk again
waiting for some thing
to appear to save him
from this dream
he cannot really be
having this boiling
discharge can't
come soon enough.

The Lady Waits

The lady waits
For the people
To catch up
With the ideal
The lady waits
At the mouth
Of the last centuries'
Port of entrance
"Bring me your
Tired" etc
Few immigrants
Pass by her now
They across further south
Still she waits
Lamp held high
Guardian of the
Golden door
"Liberty and
Justice for all"
Only time will
Tell if we can
Deliver

The Liquid Daze

There was a time
in the liquid days
(seems so long ago)
when time wept unnoticed
down the face of the dripping clock.
Oh yes it was a time indeed
gone now but not
forgotten.
That time lays buried
under years of things done
like layers of silt laid down
by the slow meandering
river of life

I sometimes find a piece of
that time but it is wrapped
like an old treasure in a
blanket of sadness.
It lays in the hallow ground
and in the twilight I always find it.
Memory is like that
sometimes it's crystal
but mostly it's a thin smokey
fog that drifts across the
battlefields of the past.
That time was a bombshell
that exploded in flight
showering shrapnel
raining chunks of spinning
razor-sharp fuckup on all
my parades for years to come.

That time...

The Miracle of Birds

Do not underestimate the
miracle of birds heard
chirping on a warm
Sunday morning
while waiting for the
day to begin.

the morning chorus

early Saturday and the computer
is humming away quite nicely
laying down its blanket of
white noise

somewhere in the distance
the neighbor's dog scratches
its neck and the collar tinkles
like a Tibetan prayer bell

a bird twitters
but it is briefly eclipsed
by the mosquito-like drone
of the morning helicopter

farther in the distance
a leaf blower declares itself
as another helicopter enters
then exits, stage left
the leaf blower is joined by
a chainsaw
a crow chimes in
the cars on the street
sound like a cool wind
rushing through a pine forest

a plane buzzes low
and a siren squeals briefly

more motors wake up
more sirens   more noise
a litany of warning
and chaos

I go back to that forest again
perhaps it is in Tibet
perhaps there is a young
boy entranced by the sounds
of his world
dreaming lazily
about the wonders of this
thing called
Nintendo.

The New Adventure – Aug. 2008

Sherman split Georgia
Like a ripened peach
Putin drove deep into
Georgia to make
A cobbler of democracy
Or so we are told
(Is there more to this
Than we can see/know?)

The sanctity of the word
Democracy
Blinds us to abuses
In its name

Democracy
As a concept
Is not a desired ideal for most
Even here in the USA
Too much mucking about
With the common 'misconception'
The misguided belief that
God is on our side and
We can do no wrong

Democracy
Is a most important word
A word beyond question
Sacred word
Word without meaning
Because the word has been
Cheapened by sham
& greed
The word or wor(l)d
Means nothing

It is nothing
As are we

(We had so much &
We gave it up
So easily)
Now it's a source of
endless sadness

The Olympics

The impure elite
Demand purity
From the average man

Doping be damned
Countries demand
Victory

Standing tall on
The necks of
Those innocents

Who strive to be
The best of
Humankind

Not of country
Nor region
Nor countryman

The Pin Cushion

The pain does not lick
Across my bones
Like a wildfire

No

Instead it punctuates
Every movement
Like a tiny hot poker or
A needle slowly tattooing
A map across my landscape of skin

I am a Mercator map
A plan for pain and destruction
Burning my bridges
One vein at a time

Nerves dying
Millimeter upon
Millimeter
Slowly creeping
Up each leg

One red dot
After another

In my mind's eye
Each dot is a town
Abandoned along
This desolation
Road
This pin cushion

The Poet from El Paso

It was great to hear
From you, greater
Still reminiscing
About those good
Old, bad old days
That we all have had
In some way or another

And thanks for your
Comments regarding
Certain poets and their
Proclivity towards BS

I'm looking for a really
Big shovel to send to
That someone special
That I mentioned to you

But I should apologize
To you as I wasn't
Exactly one hundred
Percent present
I did a fair job of
Getting it done but I
Could have been a
Little more on the ball

As I said
It was a real pleasure
Shooting the shit
With you and I hope
We can get together
Again soon

The Quiet Revolution

Reading the definitive words
From the mouth of the self-
Proclaimed revolutionary
It always comes back to
Who has legitimate claim
To the bragging rights:
Sex drugs/booze and the quest
For the perfect poem

The young will dream
About doing what the old
Half-remember doing but the
Truth is lying somewhere
In the middle
Waiting to straddle
Or be straddled

If you believe what is written
Poetry is nothing but a cheap whore
To which we all must pay homage

However if you ignore what is written
And remember that poetry is the
Miracle of small things made large
Then you will continue to celebrate
That notion in your own quiet
And persistent way
Perhaps even
With some success.

The Road To Ruin

It's a two way street
the road to ruin
but no one seems to know this
Or perhaps
they choose instead
to ignore
this knowledge
because it's so much easier
to pretend that someone else
is doing the leading.

When your life lays in ruins
and you can't think straight
when you're mind is discombobulated
and cobwebs and other dusty crap is raining
down
from some roof beam overhead
and the world doesn't make any sense at all
and the walls are undulating
and you wish that they would just close in
and be done with it
these are the times where
you look for an answer to your dilemma
You look outside your own window
but there isn't usually any reason or rhyme
to explain why
you are
so
fucked
up...

The road to ruin
like the road to Hell
it's paved with ground up human bones
and grouted with the blood and guts
of generations of excuses
It's the answer to the question
Life
Death
and the whole ball of wax.

The Seed Lady

She comes in colors,
metaphor
and signs
a crooked smile
she is an interpretive dance
an ode to meaning

Her bag of seeds
clarifies the wisdom of
your daze
an organic tarot
she suggests
not future or past
but who you are
now
what you are
now

It's not gris gris
or voodoo
but a literal
translation
of meaning
of vision
the zen seed

difficulty
erased
reality
questioned
mind
full
relationships

The Siren's call

reaching out to me like a lifeline
hurled into the frothing
angry sea
towards the drowning man

Come and spread your wings over me
scoop me up and carry me away
from this churning maelstrom
from this hate-filled
cityscape
take me beyond
reason's grasp
beyond passion's lofty heights
absorb me into your
perfect blackness
at last!

The Sloop

Sailboats in a marina
Glassy night waters
Sound of hulls
Rubbing against docks
Halyards snapping
Against masts
In the distance
The buoy that marks
The mouth of the harbor
Tolls its warning

I was a seventeen year old runaway
Seeking refuge onboard
The sloop owned by my father
It was so many years ago
I don't even remember
The boat's name
Except that it was made by Slavi Larsen

It was a beautiful boat with
Teak decks and mahogany trim
Wooden hull, wide in the beam
A big slow weekend "cruiser"
Not designed for racing

I loved that boat
It was something
Solid in my life
Even though it was
In constant motion

There was something
Comforting about
Being aboard her
Hiding out from
The world
No screaming
No terror
Just the quiet slap
Of water against the hull
As if the ocean was saying
"There, there, you're safe for now"

The Soon To Be Rapture

Mingus on the box
And Kerouac
Freshly resting
On my brow
With such fine
Company
What man wouldn't
Find a way
To make this
Lazy afternoon
Pass slower?

Mingus racing
Up and down the
Neck of that up-
Night bass like a
Crazy game of tag
While Dolphy (Eric)
Unraveled the sweet
Here-after mysteries
Of Space and Time
Using an alto sax
Like a divining rod -
Searching for a "now"
Interpretation, a
New constant by
Which we will all
Live as one in the
Soon to be rapture.

And Kerouac (Jack)
With bony fingers
No longer gripping
Reality with one hand

On the stick shift
And one on the wheel
Is he cruising the road
In an eternal midnight
Memory meltdown
From inside his tomb
Or from the steps
Of some nirvana just
Over the border near
Juarez or Jalisco?

And what of Neal
(My favorite) the
Real deal? What would he say to
us now, ancient
words or back-hand-
ed 'fuck you's?
Is it hard to think
With a head that
Looks like a flat-
Ened penny? Isn't it
Neal? All gone you
Say? All gone &
Just worms and
Muck left behind
As if to say "yeah,
We're done here,
Man, what's next?"

What IS next?
Armageddon?
Gloria and chaos?
6 inches of 'hot'
or 8 inches of 'ho-

> > >

hum'? Won't
Matter anyway
The days are out-
Numbered by the
Sad faces of history.

We will all miss
The songs of the
Birds soon enough.

The Wages of Living

My father always acted as if he was embarrassed
by us kids
as if we were a part of his secret life
as if we were the side effects
of a marriage he wasn't ever sure
he wanted to be in.
Seventeen years into it
he knew it was wrong
that we were wrong for him
So he left
and took up with one of my mom's best friends.

It's funny, now that I think about it
But, of course, it wasn't so funny back then

The Watcher

Turning ideas over in my head like jagged rocks
turning them over and over until they
become round and rough
like sandblasted marbles
turning them over still
until they are smooth
and featureless and most of all
safe
as safe as pebbles in a reflecting pool
as safe as a darkened theater
as safe as shadows
as safe as a world glimpsed through
a slit in a door

The watcher is a stranger
the visitor who never returns home
the tourist with no return ticket

The Wolf At The Door

Destiny waits in the hallway
It waits patiently knowing
I will have to open the door
To take out the trash some day
Knowing that I'm waiting
Patiently behind the door
All fang and claw and hairy paw
To get in the first shot.

Destiny gives fate a call and
Fate smiles an Ed McMahon
Happy meal smile at destiny's
Plan of attack and I feel a
Burning sensation on my ears

Is that the full moon coming
To the rescue?

The World According to Diabetes

"Well, at least you still have your twenty digits!"

And how many
do you have?
Nineteen
Well, that's
better than
eighteen, I
suppose
Yes, but
it's a damn
sight worse
than
twenty!

The Young Poet

The young poet
Gives his wife a
Wink and a nod
Some of us turn
She glows with
A demure whole-
Someness that I'm
Not used to seeing

The young poet
Knows who is
Responsible for
This as he rocks
Gently to and fro
Savoring this mo-
Ment his wife
Smiling from the
Back wall of the
Coffee bar

The young poet
May be cocky now
But he doesn't know
That I can still
Remember when
I was called to repair
The slats on his
Bed which were
Busted out in the
Usual way...

Too much
Bouncing

Things I Notice #8

"It's too early for the circus, it's too late for the bars..."
—Tom Waits

Unable to sleep
I open the door into
The 2 a.m. chill and
Lean out
The night is quiet
Save for one bird
Tweeting out an
Extended solo
Over the muffled
Roar of the ocean
In the distance
But really it's
The near eternal
Rush of traffic
Pulsing like
Ocean waves
Crashing on
The beach
Somewhere
It's funny
I've lived
Near the
Ocean for
A half century
Now and I've
Not heard the
Crash of the
Waves since Reagan
Yet I clearly
Can recall
What it

Sounds
Like
I inhale this
Moment
Exhale and
Close the
Door
In bed
Writing
I'm suddenly
Very tired
And ready
For sleep
At last

Tonight It's the Russian Children

The pawns get younger and younger
In the eternal chess match
Between 'good' and 'evil'
Tonight it's some children
Who are victims

I saw them
On telemundo
Half-naked
Running
Like scared rabbits
Innocent martyrs
Of Russia's own war
On terror

God knows what
Russia did to
Provoke this
It must have been
Too terrible to
Show

Even on
Telemundo

Touch Me

Touch me
and let the masks fall
from my harlequin face
like leaves collecting
at winter's doorstep.

Touch me
and unleash reluctant tears
as an uneasy rain
to absolve my sins
and wash away my
memories
of this paradise lost.

Touch me
and make me whole
my darling.

Touch me

TOUGH

And yet
Not really

I'm a loner
Sure
I like to be
In a crowd of
Friends
Engaging in
Delightful
Repartee
But I'm still
A loner
At heart
And even as
The precious world of
Who did what
To whom
I'm still aware of
The cotton-candy
Insulation that
Protects me from
Being in their world

I've made it this far
But really
It's been more
Luck than bravado
More "oops" than
Tough old motherfucker

Sure
I've made it this
Far on something that
Passes for guts
But I am really not
The bad boy that
Rumor has it
I'm just a guy
Tryin' to get
Through the night
/ day
To the next gig

Yet I'm seen as a
Thug
Perhaps somewhat
Lovable but still
A thug

Yet what self-respecting
Thug cries while watching
"Extreme Home Makeover" or
"It's a Wonderful Life"

Tran Zen Dance

The beer can arcs into the bed of the truck with a simple grace
as if it has always been arcing
always been doing this
taking this trip
riding the rainbow over and into the bed
of the truck
a moment of perfect symmetry.

TYRRANUS SEXUALIS

It's been raining for too many days
I mean-Christ! if I wanted this kind of weather I would
move to Seattle or Oakland
or some damned place
But, like I said
it's been raining for too many days in a row
When it rains like this
I always get a little edgy
maybe it's all the negative ions
or something, I don't know
Anyway
I was eating breakfast today
huddled at the counter
when I saw an ex-girlfriend of mine
ensconced in a booth
in the corner with a guy who
I assumed was her new man
(they were kissing and looking deeply into each others eyes)
and I remembered, briefly, how she had done that with me
and then I quickly looked away.
I had moved too fast with her
was too easily taken in by what she had said
I believed her when she said:
"You're mine, Raindawg!"

She was trouble
I saw it
my friends saw it
they warned me, but I ignored them
The next thing I know
I'm on the street again
doing the solo number.

> > >

And what was the sticking point?
Sex.
As usual.
She'd offer it up but yank it away before I could
get more than a taste.
So there I was
thinking with the wrong head
playing with the wrong organ
a monkey on a chain
dancing for chump change
While she played me like the fool I am.
For what?
For a brief whoopee?
One more trip to the well?
One more brief encounter of the best/worst kind?

It's not just sex that I crave
it's the yielding that occurs during good sex
the blending of souls that happens
when you let your guard down
with someone you
don't even know all that well
It's much more profound than
mere vulnerability
It's more like merging
with the divinitine
Becoming one with the godhead.
This is what I crave.
The sex is just a vehicle I ride in
on my way to another state of being.
Don't get me wrong
I'm not snooty about sex

I'd rather ride in the downy folds to the seat of nirvana
than sit cross-legged staring at a candle
chanting a mantra.
I'm just saying that sex lets me
intertwine with the oneness-
the cosmic glue that holds the entire universe
together.

Plus it feels really good.

Unnamed Act

Fiona Apple drops into the room
her words oozing down white walls
streaked with shadows

I sit in a room with simple decor
unassuming and delicate
with a hint of possibility

Unaccustomed to this infusion of
morning light, sitting at this table
in this artist's life, a stranger
passing through yet another room
on my way to a point beyond the
horizon

I blindly trust that the point will be there
when I, too, move beyond the view.

These simple rooms that speak volumes in their understated grace
The photographer's vision, like a poet's, depends on light and interpretation
But I fear that once the novelty of this light wears off
I will rush back to the soft cushion of darkness
that I could not ignore my shaking hand now visible in the light of day
that these bright rooms would contrast deadly to my bleak soul-scape
my season of bleakness, like an unending winter
that the act
the unnamed act
would call to me
call me to take the final steps

The edge beckons always, like the promise of a lost love's return.

Unleashing the Hounds

Someone once
Told me that
We had to invade
Iraq not for WMD
But to end the
Reign of the Butcher
Of Baghdad

Now the dogs of war
Notwithstanding
It seems to me that
We have unleashed the
Butchers of Baghdad
And nothing will stop
The carnage until
There is no one left
Standing

I wonder if that person
Is proud of the fine
Can of worms that
We have opened
yet again

Untitled

On the occasion of watching
The twenty-fifth anniversary
Of the Ken Burns Civil War
Documentary contemplating
The stupid excess of carnage
I suddenly remembered this
Moment in San Pedro at the
House on Shepard Street

I sat on the edge of the sofa
Playing a song I had written
For you with such heartache
And feeling that the woman
I was attempting to impress
Was taken aback and said
I see that your heart is still
Taken by the ghost of your
Past

Of course she was right I
Knew it would never work
But I tried anyway and lost

Still I regret her loss though
Not as much as your loss but
Still
At least
She played a fine fiddle

untitled 2

Big Motherfucking Cockroach
runs click   click
clicking off tempo
across the kitchen floor
while I'm working
on a funky guitar riff.

I think
look motherfucker
we have to share this
place
at least you
could get the fucking
tempo right.

Untitled 3

Sunflower:
Crazy painter
Bread & sardines:
Crazy poet
Fire hydrant:
Crazy bus driver
Blue ball:
Crazy universe

Uprooted

In loving memory for Holly and a time in a land called Peedro.

The gypsy highway calls
hypnotically
she beckons to me
with strange and exotic
sounding words
that are meaningless to me
indiscernible

something moves
inside me as
she rosins up the bow
and fiddles with my
heart strings

Ah! at last I understand!

a moment
remembered
vanishing as fast
as a wisp of smoke.

Vacation

I'm trying to sleep in someone else's bed
It's not as easy as they thought it would be
Where I sleep, what I'm used to
it's more like a crypt that I crawl into
dark and cold with pillows like stones
my mattress is hard and flat, like a pallet
My windowless cell, with it's barred skylight
my dank prison calls to me to turn away
from the comforts of white walls, early morning light,
pale curtains and a wall furnace that happily
churns out heat as I stand naked in predawn chill
marveling at the thin red line panorama:
Eastern mountains cloaked in blue,
a silver sliver of moon hung in pale blue-gray sky
the sea, an oily gun-metal blue.

It's hard to believe that I'm still in the same town.

Water

Is life
We take it for granted
It forms the bulk of our beings
Without it we will die
Our crops will die
Life as we know it
Will cease
Water is the new oil
It is our definition of a good life
We search for signs of it
On other planets
And rejoice when we think
We find evidence of it
Yet we corrupt it with
Chemicals and other
Pollutants here
On the only world
I will ever call home

What Unites Us

The need to feel like
You are a human being
Is universal
Whether you are trying
To make ends meet
In Baghdad
Tehran
Haifa
Basra
Tripoli
Paris
Belfast
Detroit
South Central
Birmingham
West Oakland
Riverside
Or even Long Beach

That is what unites us
This longing to be treated
As if our *lives* matter

Witness

I am a witness
To all that is the
Wonder and
Disgrace of
This life or what
We call life
This life
My life
Your life
Our life

Sometimes this life
Is almost unbearable
What we do to each
Other in the name of
Some thing or some
God or some ideal
And

Sometimes this life is
A complete surprise
Because of what we
Do to each other in
The name of some
Thing or some God
Or some ideal

II.

I am a witness to the
Crimes that men and
Women do to each
Other in the name of
Love or possession it's

> > >

Never clear until the
Dust settles and then
It's too late

I see how you position
Your body when you
Sit down across from
Me as if I was a thief
Who has come to steal
Your charms

But I am not a thief as I
Do not make a move on
Your charms or your
Vulnerabilities or your
Fair skin or your Raven
Hair as wild as any
River or wind-swept sea

No you have me confused
I am not a thief I will not
Steal your heart or your
Children's dreams or yours
In the dead of night I will
Not make a move on you
I am here to observe and
Protect where possible

I am a witness and perhaps
More important I am a
Friend – please don't forget
That I am observing this life
My life your life our life now
You are dancing because it's

All you can do that makes any
Sense in this crazy free-for-all

God it's hard watching you
Dance these intricate steps
You glide without effort
Like a great roiling river
You are a force of nature
Even if you can't see it
Trust me I have seen many
People who had this magic

I am a witness after all
I know my business

You

It's odd when you look at the facts:
a long day's drive from here, you are gardening
and scratching your dog's ears
but you might as well be across the country or in another
dimension where I can't touch you, except by phone.

The cartoon anvil that dropped from the stratosphere
the day you drove out of town
has just made its way back to ground zero.
The powers have decided that the spot that will be marked by that particular "X" today
will be located on the roof above my apartment
just above where I was sitting, innocently, like a picnicker at Bull Run
thinking it would all be over in a split second.
I was half-right.
The impact was over in a nano-second
but the repercussions, like waves sloshing in a pool, are many.
The anvil, making a cameo appearance in this way-off Broadway play:
"This is your life, buddy-boy", dropped in for a visit on my only day off this week.
It hit hard pushing me down deep into its "footprint".
Now I'm flatter than I've been in a long long time
a mere shadow looking for my lost self to re-attach to.

Come home now
reunite my shadow with myself.

ZEN-FUCK-YOU

The Human Being is prone to a self-imposed oblivion

Aware of the impending downfall
the days begin to slip away from me
in a defiance of logic :
The lesson of History is those who do not learn from the mistakes of the past
       must repeat them
implying that death is inevitable until we figure otherwise
that despite our best intentions and efforts all that we know and love and hate
will be so much dust after our passing
The legacy of all my days will neither serve nor hinder the passage of time
nor alter the seasons
nor rearrange the stars
But I could be wrong

and it's in the believing of that that keeps me in the dilemma

Is life really just a conveyor belt
that dumps us into the great belching fire-breathing
mouth of an uncaring eternity?
Are we just bouncing along heading into the wind
supposing that some act or another will be immortalized
and that somehow we will cheat death in some small way
perhaps living beyond our oh-so-finite span.

All this I deduced while watching the "parade"
down sixth street. Poetry in motion as life unfolds
Saturday morning, the jazz is thumping
the biggest cat in the whole world resides in the window
(what's he thinking about?)
Trees shimmer, their leaves massaged by something called wind
(what is that, anyway?)
The red awning enshrines the law office (378) next to the Japanese
Restaurant that rejects oriental philosophy (Senfuku)

                                                                     > > >

The glass mirrors the traffic flow
cars and moving bodies merging in both directions at the point of intersection
a geometric anomaly like hate/love or fear/desire
like phone calls that turn ugly or stop making sense in mid-sentence
or like shadow-ghosts lurking just beyond the periphery of one's vision
or bad feelings over coffee
or the smells of decay and old age

I just can't get away from the rot
maybe it's being forty six and not feeling like I'm that old
and yet the fact is I am
whatever the implications are
it's inescapable
and next time I'll be forty seven and so on until the dust collects

INTERNATIONALLY RECOGNIZED poet / publisher, **RD Armstrong** aka **Raindog**, has 18 chapbooks and 9 books to his name (including several anthologies that he has edited) and has been published in over 300 poetry magazines, anthologies and e-zines. He also operates the LUMMOX Press which has published over 100 issues of the LUMMOX Journal; and nearly 200 other titles including the chapbook series, Little Red Books and the Respect perfect bound series. The LUMMOX Poetry Anthology is his most important project. Since 2012, he has been relying, mostly, on book sales to cover half of the monthly budget.

Visit the website at ***www.lummoxpress.com*** to learn how to order books… they'll look great on your book shelf after you've finished reading them! Or leave them out and impress your friends.

The **LUMMOX Press** was established in 1994
by the poet RD Armstrong.
Previous series include the Little Red Books
and the LUMMOX Journal. Currently publishing
chapbooks, a perfect bound book series,
a Poetry Anthology & Poetry Contest (annually),
and "e-copies" (PDFs) of all its books.

The goal of the press and its publisher is to
raise the bar for poetry, while bringing
the "word" to an international audience.
We are proud to offer this book
as part of that effort.

For more information and to see our
growing catalog, please go to
www.lummoxpress.com

www.ingramcontent.com/pod-product-compliance
Lightning Source LLC
Chambersburg PA
CBHW031140160426
43193CB00008B/200